The Centennial FOOD GUIDE

A CENTURY OF GOOD EATING

THE CANADIAN CENTENNIAL LIBRARY

The Centennial
FOOD GUIDE

A CENTURY OF GOOD EATING

Comprising an anthology of writings about food and drink over the past hundred years, together with divers recipes, helpful suggestions, curiosa and illustrations culled from old records, the whole being seasoned with the personal prejudices and enthusiasms of the authors ⌐ PIERRE AND JANET BERTON

THE CANADIAN CENTENNIAL LIBRARY

WEEKEND MAGAZINE / MCCLELLAND AND STEWART LIMITED

Colour photographs by Bert Bell
produced by Joan Chalmers

Pierre Berton, *Editor-in-Chief*
Frank Newfeld, *Art Director*
Ken Lefolii, *Managing Editor*

CONTENTS

Janet's SOUP

The male editor of this book unconditionally guarantees this soup. In twenty years of marriage he has drunk bathtubfuls of it. Moreover he has never seen anyone content with but a single bowl. It demands seconds, thirds and even fourths, which is why we urge that it be made in vast quantities. Here's how:

Take *1 large beef heart*, place it in a pot with four quarts of cold water, bring to a boil and skim. Take all the leaves and tops from *4 celery stalks* plus *3 large onions*, finely chopped, and simmer with the heart for two days. Remove meat and vegetables and strain the broth. To this add the following vegetables, finely diced:

4 stalks celery, 2 carrots, ½ turnip, ¼ green pepper, ¼ cup parsley, ½ cup chives.

Then pour in *2 large tins tomatoes* and add these herbs and condiments:

1 tsp. each of oregano, celery seed, marjoram, thyme, basil and monosodium glutamate; ½ tsp. each of sage, savory, rosemary and chervil. Dash of Tabasco sauce, Angostura bitters and Worcestershire sauce. Salt, pepper to taste.

Now cook the soup for half an hour and serve. The aroma is maddening. The flavour intoxicating. A little dry bread should be its only companion. It is a meal in itself.

For future meals remove all vegetables and strain again. Then add one half cup each of freshly diced celery, carrots and onions. Bring to a boil but don't cook the vegetables further. Serve.

The soup improves with age. As it simmers on the back of the stove the water in which other vegetables have been cooked may be added to it. If this makes the stock too thick simply strain and start again.

And don't throw out that beef heart. It can be converted to Shepherd's Pie (see p. 8) or stuffed with bread crumbs, onions, celery and all the condiments listed above, baked in a 325° oven for half an hour and served as a main dish with baked potatoes.

On Tribal Feeding

It's a truism in our house that my husband married me because he discovered I like my steak *bleu*. I was raised that way and so was he and though we argue about a lot of other things we don't argue about food. We both like our breakfast eggs boiled soft and light and we refuse to mingle socially with those who insist on prying them out of the shell after they've been rendered rubbery. We like our toast burned to a dark brown. We like our bacon thin and very crisp, with every slice laid out separately in the pan, cooked till its toes turn up, and drained well on a piece of absorbent paper. We cannot *stand* mushy vegetables in our soups and we hate all bland foods except things like artichokes, eggplant and Belgian endive. We like curry in our chowder and fresh lime juice on our curry and plenty of oregano in almost everything. We like textures in our food – something crispy at every meal and something slippery, too. And we like colour: I'd never dream of serving three green vegetables; at least one would have to be red and another, hopefully, yellow or orange or white or purple. Moreover there's almost nothing we don't like to eat and absolutely nothing we won't try once.

We try to bring up our children the same way: In spite of a depressing leaning towards sandwiches made of peanut butter and cheap strawberry jam, I believe we're succeeding. One of them came home the other day and complained that the food she'd eaten at somebody else's place was tasteless, which is another way of saying they don't use enough herbs and spices. Another, aged five, gobbled up all the smoked octopus her father was preparing to nibble at with his pre-dinner cocktail. Sometimes we both wish they'd stick to peanut butter and jam.

I have seven children to cook for, plus Pierre, and for this reason, if no other, I've become used to making do with every scrap. In our house nothing gets thrown away. Vegetable juices left over from cooking are popped into a waiting pot of soup on the stove or served with herbs, hot, as a pre-dinner drink. (Try spinach juice, lightly flavoured with a little lemon, some salt and pepper and a dash of thyme next time; it's delicious.) Vegetable peelings and hulls go to the compost heap in the garden to help grow more vegetables next year. Left-over meat scraps are made into hash or

ECONOMICAL SHEPHERD'S PIE

This is the pie made from the beef heart used in the soup on page 7. Sauté **1 onion**, chopped, in butter. Add **3 stalks celery**, chopped. Chop the beef heart into small pieces and add to the sautéed vegetables in the bottom of a buttered casserole. Thicken with a little flour. Add ½ **tsp. oregano**, ½ **tsp. thyme**, ½ **tsp. marjoram**, ½ **tsp. Worcestershire sauce**, plus **salt**, **pepper** and **monosodium glutamate** to taste. Pour in enough of the stock from the heart (used in the soup) to moisten or, failing that, tomato juice or diluted beef fluid. Cover with a layer of **cooked mashed potatoes** and cook in a 350° oven for 45 minutes.

shepherd's pie. I make a lot of very good soup stock from beef heart, as the original recipe on page 7 indicates, but when the heart has been wrung dry of its juices, it's still valuable. You can stuff it or you can make shepherd's pie out of it.

As for old bones, we *never* throw them away. Pierre likes

soup three or four times a day and I usually have two or three kinds brewing, many of them made from old bones. It's got to be a kind of joke around our place – but one that my children take seriously. Recently, when the two of us were away for the weekend we left our five little ones in the care of our two eldest daughters, aged fifteen and seventeen. The girls took the whole kit and caboodle on a fried-chicken picnic to a boy friend's summer cottage some fifty miles away. To the astonishment of their hosts they carefully wrapped up all the gnawed chicken bones and brought them home again. When we returned late Sunday night there was a pot of spiced chicken broth bubbling away on the stove.

LEFTOVER CHICKEN BROTH

Simmer all the gnawed **chicken bones** your family ate for dinner. (We know this can't be done in restaurants because of the department of health but there **is** a certain amount of togetherness in most families and besides, the hot water does kill the germs.) It's best to leave the bones on a small burner to simmer for a day or two, or until you get time to make the soup. Add **celery leaves** and any wilted celery you have around to the soup; just chuck it in–don't bother to chop it. Add just a trace of **onion** and also the **giblets of the chicken** if you didn't put them in the gravy. Cook until the bones are white and clean. Strain the soup. Add **salt, pepper** and **monosodium glutamate** to taste and at the last minute some finely chopped **celery**. Cook the celery just enough to tenderize it but not so it will lose all its crunchiness. Serve with a **slice of lemon** on top and a sprig of fresh **parsley**.

Sometimes, of course, you can carry the leftover mania too far. I remember once a childless couple, newly arrived in Toronto from New York, came out for dinner a week after Christmas. I served them a rich turkey soup and they found it hard to believe that it was made from the same Christmas turkey they had helped us eat the week before. They'd never made soup in their lives before, since there were only two of them, but they certainly intended to try: When we visited their apartment a month later the refrigerator was bulging with small paper bags full of scraps. "Damn it – all I get to eat now is frozen garbage!" the husband complained.

The secret, of course, of making do with leftovers is in using herbs and spices. We even grow some, though that can sometimes be a problem if you've got only a small garden. Sage, which is one of the handsomest of all leafy plants, being a soft, grey blue, and one of the finest herbs to use fresh, has a habit of taking over a perennial border. It almost took over us one year until my husband regretfully dug it all up. I took about a pound of the fresh leaves and crammed them into a whole chicken which I then roasted to a turn. The fresh sage permeated the fowl, giving it a flavour that is indescribable. Try it some time.

My three eldest daughters are all good cooks and love practising in the kitchen. I find it's a lot easier on everyone just to let them go ahead when they're learning. I start them out by showing them where the recipe books are and letting them go to it. It's more fun for them and easier on me and sometimes we make an exciting food discovery. The worst that can happen is that the kitchen gets into a mess–but then when Father cooks the mess is really terrible. He loves to chop things – onions and green peppers mostly for his

scrambled eggs – and when he chops the floor is soon knee deep in peelings.

PIERRE'S SCRAMBLED EGGS

Chop very fine **1 large green pepper, 2 onions** and **1 lb. sliced bacon.** Sauté in ¼ **lb. butter.** Add **1 tbsp. curry powder** to the mixture as it cooks. While it is cooking chop up **1 apple,** fine, and **2 large tomatoes.** When the onions are very soft add the apple and tomatoes together with **1 tsp. black pepper, 1 tsp. oregano, 1 tsp. Worcestershire sauce, 2 tsps. monosodium glutamate,** a dash of **Tabasco sauce** and salt to taste. Add ½ **cup dry white wine.** Allow this mixture to simmer while breaking **1 doz. eggs** into a bowl. Add **1 tbsp. dry mustard** and **2 cups milk** to the eggs. Stir in the mustard well. Now pour the contents of the bowl into the mixture simmering in the pan. As it coagulates prevent it from burning by stirring bottom of the pan with a fork. When it has congealed but is still soft serve at once on hot plates. Serves 6 hungry people.

I'm strong for children striking off on their own. I remember once when my daughter Penny, then eleven, was visiting her grandmother she was allowed to *help* at making a cake. She balked; it was no fun just to help with the beating when she'd been allowed to undertake the whole operation at home. I think children get much more of a sense of accomplishment when they find out how to flavour things for themselves instead of blindly following the recipe. The essence of cooking, surely, lies in the tasting and I encourage my daughters to taste their way into a recipe. That's why I had so much trouble writing down my recipe for vegetable soup for this book. I'd never before actually measured any of the ingredients. I simply keep tasting until the soup is right.

I couldn't cook at all at Penny's age, though I used to watch my mother who is a wonderful cook. I remember one afternoon when I was about sixteen, my friend Dorothy and I had the house to ourselves and so decided to make some simple blanc mange. We found a recipe, followed the directions faithfully and when it was finished put it in the ice box in some little serving dishes. When mother came home she tasted it, made a wry face and remarked that we hadn't cooked it enough. "Cook it!" we cried. "We didn't cook it at all. It didn't *say* to cook it!" And sure enough, it didn't. I guess the authors of that cookbook naturally assumed that everyone would know enough to cook raw starch, but we didn't. That's why some of the old school home economics texts are good for beginners though I must say some of them are pretty dull when it comes to adventurous flavourings.

I didn't really learn to cook until three friends and I found a scarce apartment in Vancouver during the war and moved from our respective boarding houses. We learned the hard way, by practice, taking turn-about a week at a time and sticking faithfully to a weekly five-dollar budget. On one memorable day Elinor served up a *pièce de résistance*, as she called it – creamed onions; we'd eaten half of them before we discovered they weren't onions at all but tulip bulbs purchased from the grocery store in error. "Well, they *looked* like onions!" said Elinor. It was during this period that my husband got the three of us tipsy on a single bottle of wartime beer by inventing the beer nog that appears on page 63. I haven't had one since but I do remember that it was delicious – and that's about all I remember.

I used to woo him in those days by serving him thick juicy steaks cooked *bleu*; but my Aunt Margaret, whose apartment I used, really did most of the cooking. I didn't yet trust myself with a man of such determined tastes.

Now twenty years and seven children later I think I can cope with almost anything. I suppose the acid test came when Pierre's New York publisher, Alfred Knopf, an international gourmet of positively terrifying proportions, visited us for lunch one hot July day just a few days before the birth of my fourth child. I had learned enough about gourmets to know that a true gourmet meal is generally a very simple, if exquisite one. So I served only three dishes, none of them too fancy but all of them requiring care.

First, I made a light lemon borscht, which I served ice cold in a tall glass *on the rocks* topped with sour cream and drunk through straws.

BORSCHT ON THE ROCKS

Peel and chop **6 beets** (or enough to fill about 3 cups). Simmer in **1 qt. soup stock** (made from beef soup bones) with **2 onions**, chopped, and **1 cup cabbage**, chopped. When the vegetables are tender, strain, and add **salt, pepper, monosodium glutamate** to taste, plus **1 tsp. celery salt** and **1 tbsp. lemon juice.** Chill and serve in very tall glasses over ice cubes, with **sour cream** topping. Drink through a straw.

Secondly, I made a lamb kebab, using very young spring lamb and taking the actual meat from the hearts of lamb chops that

I marinated overnight. This, skewered with mushroom caps, small onions and small firm tomatoes, was roasted on a barbecue grill so hot that the lamb was slightly charred on the outside but light pink in the centre.

MARINADE FOR LAMB KEBAB

Mix **1 cup red wine** with **1 cup olive oil, 3 cloves garlic**, chopped, **1½ tsp. thyme** and **1½ tsp. marjoram.** Marinate overnight. When the kebabs are cooking on skewers, with onions, green peppers, mushrooms and small firm tomatoes, baste continually with the marinade.

Finally I served a dish of fresh raspberries in kirsch. And, of course, French drip coffee. Mr. Knopf is not a man who indulges in flattery or hyperbole so when he later told my husband that it was the best meal he'd had in Canada, I was delighted.

Another interesting meal was the one I served to the Finnish architect who designed the Toronto city hall, Viljo Revell, who came to dinner with his wife. Since they were newly arrived in Canada I thought it would be fun to give them an all-Canadian meal. We served one similar to the one on page 105 but with certain differences. Oysters Canadian had not then been invented; Pierre and I concocted those in the summer of 1965 especially for this book, using pigweed and dandelions from our own weed patches. And the main dish was not Brome Lake duckling but roast young buffalo fresh from the annual government kill at Wainwright. Few Canadians know that it can be purchased annually through their butcher if he can find out which packer has been favoured that year with the franchise to sell it. The government is looking to the day when buffalo meat will be a Canadian staple and there's no reason, in my mind, why it shouldn't be. Personally, I find it just as good as beef – a little richer perhaps – and I cook it exactly the same way, though being very lean it requires extra basting. I usually put a little red wine in my basting mixture.

We feed a lot of visitors at our house because we live a long way from the city and people need strength to get back home again. We believe in only two kinds of parties: small, intimate dinners or very large bashes with lashings of hearty food and some kind of crazy punch.

Our sit-down dinners are rarely for more than eight people. Usually we try to serve dishes that we've encountered at some restaurant in some corner of the world and would like to try out. If we can't get the recipe we simply use our eyes and our brains and do our best to copy – quite often successfully. That's how we arrived at the dinner shown on page 120. The lemon soup we discovered in a Persian restaurant in New York. Pierre invented the pepper steak himself as a result of watching waiters in Soho restaurants in London prepare it at his table. The deep-fried camembert came as a result of a gourmet dinner in Toronto's Franz Josef Room: we got the recipe from the chef there – it's a German appetizer. The stuffed tomatoes and the dilled cucumber salad I've been making for years.

At our large parties we have as many as seventy guests and here the trick is to serve a palatable but easily made drink that can be ladled out by the gallon and hearty food that can be eaten in the hands. We often make a good wine and brandy punch, especially for

hot weather outdoor parties, and you'll find the recipe for it on page 47. At these big barbecues we usually cook three or four of the rolled porterhouse roasts that are shown, complete with the herbal filling on page 92. They are expensive but if you can afford to splurge there's nothing better. They slice easily and cleanly and each slice can be laid between two pieces of crusty French bread. The meat, which should be well hung, is tender enough to eat in such a sandwich without knife and fork. If there's one thing we hate it's the balancing act that takes place at so many of those suburban buffets when the wretched guests are asked to cope with casserole, salad, scalloped potatoes and garlic bread – all on one knee.

In the winters we sometimes have a sleighing party and when that happens Pierre usually makes the baked beans – which are based on the kind he was raised on in the Klondike but to which he has added certain ingredients of his own, such as sherry, French mustard and tabasco sauce. A good thing to serve with these beans – though, really, you scarcely need anything else except bread and butter – is a haunch of ham, hot, or an entire roast suckling pig. After a sleighing party we find people are pretty hungry, especially if they've been drinking our hot rum. Besides a spoonful of butter and another of honey or maple syrup in our mug of rum, we add two spoonfuls of lemon juice and four spices: a dash each of cloves, ginger, cinnamon and nutmeg.

I have a theory about the preparation of food: I think you get a lot more food for the starving soul out of preparing an interesting meal and putting a lot of your own work into it. That's one reason why we don't use the instant type of food in our house. The other is that my husband simply refuses to countenance

mixes of any kind. Frankly, I think he's right. Unless you've got a job and have to make every second count, then it's much better to go in for the long slow-cooking methods. I don't think any mix or powder does the job as well as the real thing and that goes for coffee, too! If I served instant coffee to my husband, I really think he'd divorce me. As for serving it to friends – well, we think it's the worst insult you can offer a guest, this implicit suggestion that he isn't worth the five minutes it takes to make a good cup of coffee.

Another thing: I don't think it's possible to cook in a vacuum – not for me, at any rate. I cook for my husband and when he's not at home I find myself making do with peanut butter sandwiches or the equivalent. But when he's coming home – on time! – I try to make an event out of a meal. I sometimes like to serve him a small fish course before the meat – a few smelts, for instance, grilled in flour and butter or a small portion of devilled crab *au gratin*, baked in a sea-shell, a dish I learned to cook when we lived in Vancouver.

DEVILLED CRAB

Sauté **1 tsp. onion**, chopped fine, **2 tbsps. celery**, chopped fine, **1 tbsp green pepper**, chopped fine, in **2 tbsps. butter**. Thicken with **2 tbsps. flour**. Add **1 cup milk** plus **salt** and **pepper** to taste and a dash each of **mustard**, **Worcestershire sauce**, **cayenne**, and **monosodium glutamate** to taste. Fold in **2 cups crab meat**, fresh if possible, or otherwise tinned. Pour the mixture into buttered shells, sprinkle with **grated cheese** and dot with butter. Brown under the broiler until the mixture becomes bubbly. Serve at once. Should serve 4 as a starter dish before soup.

On weekends, especially, when there's time to enjoy good food, we like to eat well: even breakfast can take on a festive air. I'd say breakfast is probably the dullest meal in Canada, though that wasn't always so – as we discovered when we did our homework on hotel breakfasts in the mid-Victorian years. Not enough people these days experiment with breakfast fish: finnan haddie in cream, for instance, as Canadian a dish as ever came out of the Maritimes, or kippered herrings. I often go to the butcher for lamb's fries or small lamb's kidneys, which few people seem to bother about. They are especially good for breakfast sautéed in wine. And in the late summer no breakfast is complete in our house without slices of green tomatoes fresh from the garden, breaded and fried in the pan with the bacon.

BREAKFAST KIDNEYS

Soak **2 lamb kidneys** in cold water for 10 minutes. Slice thinly and sauté in butter for 5 minutes. Add **6 tbsps. red wine** and simmer 5 more minutes. Add a dash each of **salt, pepper, thyme, marjoram** and **monosodium glutamate**. Serve on hot buttered toast.

BREAKFAST MUSHROOMS

Slice several **large black mushrooms** fairly small and sauté them in butter. When the mushrooms are soft add several tablespoons of **red wine**. Cook in the pan until the wine has simmered down to a sauce. Serve hot on buttered toast with **salt** and **pepper**. These go well with thin, crisp bacon.

With a late Sunday morning breakfast like this you don't really need much lunch, but since everybody around our house demands it I often serve a very simple single casserole made of tomatoes, hard-boiled eggs and cheese which I also recommend, along with egg-in-the-hole, as a midnight snack.

A LATE NIGHT SNACK

Hard-boil **4 eggs**. Split lengthwise and place in a low casserole. Make a cheese sauce by melting in a bowl **2 tbsps. butter** and adding **2 tbsps. flour**, **1½ cups milk**, **1 cup cheddar cheese**, grated, and a **dash of cayenne**. Simmer sauce for a few minutes at a low heat. Slice **2 tomatoes**. Place one slice on top of each egg and pour the cheese sauce over it all. Sprinkle with paprika and bake in the oven until the cheese sauce is bubbling. Serve at once with a garnish of parsley. Serves 2 persons.

These last are very simple dishes that anyone can make. In fact, I gather that a good many pioneers made them more than a century ago, for we've found similar recipes in the old cookbooks and settlers' diaries. Indeed our researches suggest that, in spite of the old cliché about Canadian cooking being bland and dull, Canadians who really cared have generally eaten pretty well. Some of the evidence of that lies in the pages that follow.

A CENTURY OF GOOD EATING

THE EXOTIC APPLE

In this photograph, taken on one of the oldest farms in Ontario, five varieties of apples are shown. On the tree, *Northern Spy*, a good eating apple, excellent for cooking. It keeps well for winter use. In front of the jar, left, the famous *McIntosh*. On the book, *Seek-no-further*, one of our oldest varieties, an early fall sweet apple used mainly for making cider. Left of the soup bowl, the relatively modern *Delicious*, known for its delicate flavour. Far left, the smaller, older *Russet*, a good crisp apple especially fine when baked. Foreground: dried apples.

AUNT LUCY'S APPLE CUSTARD PIE

(Adapted by the authors from an 1877 recipe)

Cream ⅓ *cup butter*, ⅓ *cup sugar* and add the beaten *yolks of 3 eggs*. Stir in *2 cups applesauce* and flavour with *1 tbsp. fresh lemon juice* and a dash of *nutmeg* and *cinnamon*. Cook in an unbaked pie shell for 35 minutes at 350°, add a standard meringue, brown and serve.

APPLE SOUP

(From Mrs. Clarke's Cookery Book, Toronto 1883)

Quarter *12 large apples*. Put them in a pan with boiling water. When the soup has a strong taste of apples strain it through a hair sieve and add more water until there are about nine pints. Add *2 tbsps. sugar*, *½ lb. raisins*, first boiled until soft. Thicken with *1 tbsp. potato meal*, dissolved in a little water. Serve well chilled.

1/How Our Forefathers Fared

"Bringing in the Plum Pudding"
The Canadian Illustrated News, *December 24, 1870*

On August 28, 1863, when the Canadian colonies were beginning to stir with talk of Confederation, two intrepid British travellers – a nobleman and a doctor – having trudged, portaged, rafted and galloped across the whole of the Canadian west in the best Victorian tradition, arrived gasping at the Hudson's Bay fort of Kamloops on the Thompson River in British Columbia.

Viscount Milton and Dr. W. B. Cheadle had spent months starving on the trail, cut off from civilization. They were eager for news of the outside world, of which there was a considerable package: The Prince, God bless him, had married. The Poles had revolted.

Bismarck was threatening Denmark. The Americans were still locked in civil war. But this feast of information was not the greatest pleasure they enjoyed. Later they were to write, more than a little guiltily, that:

"The height of happiness – we say it advisedly, yet knowing the contempt which must overwhelm us: it is true, oh, philosopher, it is true, dear lady, with strong mind and spectacles, wearer of cerulean hose – the height of happiness was eating and drinking! Deal with us gently, sour ascetics and stern divines, abhorring the carnal, and corpulent, virtuous magistrates who sit in judgment on miserable creatures driven into

sin by starvation – *expertis credite*. Have we not thousands on our side in this great city who daily hunger? – not to mention a few aldermen and a well-fed bishop or two to back us on principle? Talk not to us of intellectual raptures; the mouth and stomach are the doors by which enter true delight. Mutton chops, potatoes, bread, butter, milk, rice pudding, tea and sugar: contrast dried horse-flesh and water or martens or nothing at all, with these luxuries."

Few Canadians, in those Confederation years, were forced to subsist on horsemeat, as Milton and Cheadle did. But not many rose to the gastronomic heights of the banquet which the pair were

16

later tendered in, of all places, Williams Creek in the Cariboo. Here, in a hospital ward hastily converted to a dining room ("the single unfortunate patient being veiled from sight by a sheet of green baize"), they feasted on soup, roast beef, boiled mutton and plum pudding washed down with lashings of champagne.

The *pièce de résistance* was surely the roast beef, for in many parts of Canada in those pre-refrigeration days it was as rare as champagne. The staple foods were the ones that would keep – beans, potatoes and salt pork, "the settler's sheet anchor." Nobody gave a hoot about calories and if the food was greasy, so much the better. In the cold, stinging winters, people craved fat as ravenously as a child craves chocolate. ("Many a time we have eaten great lumps of hard grease – rancid tallow used for making candles – without bread or anything to modify it.") In fact, the adjective "fat" was a term of praise among the Indians, whether applied to dog, horse or woman.

Certainly the staple prices were low enough in those days. In the seventies, fifteen cents would buy a pound of pork or a pound of butter or two dozen eggs. But cane sugar was an expensive luxury. It was the age of maple sugar and when the maple sugar was all eaten up many a farmwife made do with "punkin' sass" – a molasses-like sweetening made by boiling the juice of pumpkins for hours.

Even in the towns such delicacies as oranges, almonds, raisins and candies were rare enough to occasion comment in the papers when they were served at conversaziones. Bananas, grapefruit and other tropical delicacies were unknown until later times.

Yet in some ways it is possible that when they did eat well, the people of those days ate better than we do today. There was no such thing as a jaded appetite in the Confederation years.

Baking was done at home,

which meant that bread tasted like bread and not like *papier-mâché*. "The great loaves shaped like clumsy butterflies" that Walt Whitman noted in his diary in French Canada came hot and crusty from the ovens. In those days before jet planes and fast freezing, people enjoyed the fleeting ecstasy of fruits and vegetables in season, fresh from garden or forest. Thus it is not surprising that so many of the seasonal festivals revolved around food. There were apple-paring bees and corn-husking bees, pumpkin-slicing bees, sugaring-off parties, fruit socials and strawberry festivals. When strawberries come fresh from the patch for a brief two weeks a year, they somehow taste sweeter. It is worth having a festival over them.

Wild berries and game, which we consider a delicacy today, were staple provender for thousands. Lumberjacks ate everything from muskrat to porcupine. Settlers cured bear hams and considered black squirrels a delicacy. James Bolton, describing a barn-raising bee at the time of Confederation, wrote that "the food was wonderful – big roasts of pork or venison and sometimes bear, partridge, quail, and fish in season, with turnips and potatoes for vegetables; delicious home-made bread and buns with maple syrup; pies and puddings galore."

And there was, of course, one great delicacy that no Canadian will ever enjoy again. The settlers craved the passenger pigeon after a winter of salt pork and they ate it, fried, stewed, roasted, boiled or made into succulent hot pies. The birds were killed by the hundreds of thousands, the plump breasts and legs being soaked in brine and smoked for winter storage. "In a few homes," one pioneer's son has recalled, "the numbers of birds packed away were so great that even the dogs were sometimes fed on them." And one day the passenger pigeon was no more.

New processing techniques and the coming of the railways

changed the eating habits of the nation. By the '80s the loggers in Haliburton County, Ontario, were moving out of the pork, beans and tea era into such delicacies as rice, raisins, beef, onions and dried apples. Maple sugar was in the decline as cane sugar, refined in Canada, became cheaper. The canning industry, already flourishing below the border, began to make rapid strides in Canada and the country went off its diet of salt pork. "We use a great deal of tinned corned beef," wrote Mrs. Cecil Hall from a Manitoba farm in 1882, "and very good it is to make into such excellent hashes and curries and is so good for breakfast."

Indeed, the seeds of the instant food craze, which every gourmet and trencherman must roundly deplore, were being laid in Oakville, Ontario, where the Chisholm brothers were learning to process dehydrated cabbage, potatoes, corn, turnips and peas. Their biggest customer was the British government and soon Royal Navy men in the farthest corners of the world were eating soup made from desiccated Canadian vegetables. So rapid were the strides made in processed foods that the droll government surveyor, James Secretan, claimed to have met, during his western tour along the CPR route, a man who produced "a small lozenge out of his waistcoat pocket the size of a pea," which he insisted would turn into a lamb chop if immersed for two minutes in a cup of hot water.

We may take this lamb chop with a grain of salt but it is clear that Canadians felt they were making some progress in the art of gastronomy. Progress of a sort, no doubt, it was; but surely the real progress was psychological. As the century wore on, men and women began to write of the delights of eating, as Milton and Cheadle did, but without the guilty apologies. Little by little food for food's sake was becoming almost respectable.

EGGS
CONVENT FASHION

Boil **4 eggs** for 10 minutes. Put them in cold water. Peel and slice **1 onion**. Melt **1 oz. butter** in a frying pan, add the onion and fry white. Then add **1 tsp. flour**, mix it well, and add ½ **pint milk** till forming a nice white sauce, ½ **tsp. salt** and ¼ **tsp** pepper. When nicely done add the eggs, cut into six pieces each, crossways. Toss them up. When hot, serve on toast.

~ The Canadian Housewife's Manual of Cookery
Hamilton, Ontario, 1861

In this letter, written from Dysart, Ontario, in what is now the Haliburton tourist district, one settler describes with a kind of dogged good humour the conditions under which good, plain Canadian fare was eaten in the winter of 1864:

We had to build a log house and come into it at Christmas when the cold was so intense that the cups and saucers froze hard together whilst we were drinking our tea and a pail of water standing by the fire side would be frozen solid during the night. . . . If you were to see the children you would believe them to be really happy although they have been without shoes all winter and our fare has been of the plainest description. It has rarely ever varied from bread, pork, potatoes and tea without butter, sugar or milk. I know of one milch cow and one horse in the whole ten townships consisting of 250 thousand acres. . . .

The following brief but pithy description of a memorable Christmas dinner on the frontier was written by Charles Frederic Morrison, who found himself on the Stikine River in B.C. on December 25, 1868:

Our Christmas dinner, I remember, consisted of a young beaver stuffed like a suckling pig, which proved delicious. Lynx also makes a good stew if you do not think of cats, and squirrels make *un grand ragoût*.

W. Sherwood Fox's father arrived in the Bruce Peninsula, Georgian Bay, in April, 1872, as a young student minister, and boarded in a log farmhouse. His son later described his arrival:

A picture of his entry into this frontier household was vividly stamped on his memory by two events of the first day: as he stepped from the steamer to the shore and walked to his summer quarters a vast flock of pigeons were flying from the east to their nesting area on the Peninsula and were casting a dark, swiftly moving cloud over the land. At his very first meal, supper, he was served adult wild pigeon. At breakfast the next morning this was the main dish, and for dinner too and then again for supper; indeed, it was the only *pièce de résistance* – and a tough one at that – of each meal for the next five weeks.

A modern broadcaster and historian, Miller Stewart, has, in a CBC radio talk, left us this description of the famous "camboose" camp cooking of the Ottawa River raftsmen:

About the great fireplace in the centre, the cook ruled supreme, with his helpers, the cookies, sweating all day to keep the fire going against a huge "backlog" in the centre of the camboose. The simple cooking was done in great cast-iron kettles which swung from "cramieres" or cranes. Or in Dutch ovens whose lids were sealed with dough and buried in the hot sand and ashes. That's how they cooked the lumberman's staple food, the original pork and beans smothered in black strap molasses. Along the roads and highways of the Ottawa Valley, you will still find that the roadside stands offer "sand baked beans" in place of hamburgs or hot dogs.

One old lumberman I talked to years ago in Bobcaygeon said, "The eatin' was the meanest part – nothin' but beans, salt pork, potatoes, flapjacks and bannock. We never seen a pie, we never seen a cookie. Nothin' sweet but blackstrap. But the tea they biled in the kittles – it was real good."

In the early days, breakfast, served at 5:30, was always fried pork, flapjacks, molasses and tea. Lunch was taken into the bush by each man in a long linen bag, and was a chunk of cold salt pork, a chunk of bread – one end of this was soaked in molasses for dessert. Each man carried a tea pail and made his own tea. Supper at night was pork and beans, potatoes, bread or bannock (which was a coarse biscuit often cooked on a shovel) and molasses and tea. They say that wise cooks put spruce needles in the tea to stop scurvy. Certainly it was a rough, monotonous, and badly balanced diet to carry men through a winter of fourteen-hour work days. When the climax of the work season came – the hectic river drive of spring – with the men working knee deep in ice water, the meals were stepped up to five a day, but the menu remained the same. The rule of silence at meals, which still persists in lumber camps, dates from these days when cooking, eating, sleeping, washing-up and loafing were all done in one room by forty men. There had to be a rule of order, and the lumber camp cook was, and still is, absolute boss in his domain. One old river driver told me at Pembroke, "I've seen a five-foot cook chase the toughest bully on the Ottawa out into the snow with a red-hot frying pan for talking at the table."

In 1883, Joshua Fraser, the son of an Ottawa Valley clergyman, wrote with enthusiasm about the two staples of shantymen's meals in the Ottawa and Madawaska lumber camps: home-baked bread and beans:

And you would be amazed at the general excellence of the cooking that is done by these fellows. Where will you find such bread as is made in their immense pots, buried in and covered over by the hot ashes at the end of the *camboose*? Not a particle of the strength and fine flavour of the flour is lost by evaporation, as in the case of a stove or open oven: It is all condensed in the bread. Then it is strong and firm, and yet – and this is the mystery to me – it is light and porous as that of any first-class housewife's.

And what shall we say about the beans? They are simply *par excellence*. They are baked in the same kind of pot as the bread, the lid being hermetically sealed to the rim by dough, and then buried in the hot ashes. The beans are first thoroughly sifted, washed and boiled, and then large slices of fat pork mixed with them. The pot is then placed in its deep bed of hot ashes, and as in the case of the bread, not a breath of steam or of the essence of the bean is allowed to escape. The fat pork, becoming dissolved by the heat, and of course, neither fried nor boiled as in other processes, becomes amalgamated with the beans, and when the whole is considered sufficiently cooked, a mess is ready, which, for succulency of flavour, and savoury richness of nutrition, will completely throw in the shade the famous pottage for which Esau bartered his birthright.

Recipes from The Home Cook Book, compiled by the ladies of Toronto and chief cities and towns of Canada and published in 1877

CHICKEN AND OYSTERS

Take a young chicken and fill the inside with oysters. Place in a jar and plunge into a kettle of water. Boil for 1½ hours. There will be a quantity of gravy in the jar from the juice of the fowl and oysters; make this into a white sauce with the addition of egg, cream and a little flour and butter. Add the oysters and serve, with parsley, as a sauce for the chicken.

GOOSEBERRY CATSUP

Boil for 4 hours, **8 lbs. gooseberries** and **4 lbs. brown sugar**. Then add **1 pint vinegar**, and **2 oz. cloves** plus **2 oz. cinnamon** tied in a bag. Boil for half an hour, put in a jar and cover well. Will keep two years by occasionally scalding and adding a little vinegar and spice.

TOMATO MUSTARD

Boil for one hour **1 peck tomatoes** and **6 red peppers**. Strain through a colander and add ½ **lb. salt**, 3 tbsps. black pepper, 1 oz. ginger, 1 oz. allspice, ½ oz. cloves, 2 onions. Boil 1 hour, add ¼ lb. mustard and ½ pt. vinegar. Bottle.

TOMATO BUTTER

Take **9 lbs. tomatoes, 3 lbs. sugar, 1 pint vinegar, 3 tbsps. cinnamon, 1 tbsp. cloves** and **1½ tbsps. allspice**. Boil 3 or 4 hours until quite thick, stirring often to prevent burning.

TONGUE TOAST

Mince very fine a **cold boiled tongue**. Mix it with milk and to every ½ pint of this mixture allow the well-beaten yolks of **2 eggs**. Add **salt** and **pepper** to taste. Simmer on the stove for a minute or two and pour it over hot buttered toast.

SQUASH PIE

Dissolve **1 cup maple sugar** in a little water and stir in **2 cups strained squash**. Add **4 eggs, 2 tsps. allspice, 2 cups milk, 1 tsp. butter**, and, at the last, **2 tsps. ginger**. Bake until set. This will fill two pie shells.

A Kettledrum – The Canadian Illustrated News, *June 22, 1862*

In the Confederation years, people took their main meal or "dinner" at noon, the evening meal being "supper." But as the century progressed, the English habit of afternoon tea came more and more into vogue. In its June 22 issue of 1872, The Canadian Illustrated News pursued the subject of garden teas in which the sexes could mingle. These went by the curious and now obsolete title of "kettledrums":

Of all the meals ever invented by the wit of man, we think the supper in all its varieties, from that which furnishes delicate dishes and choice wines for a choice party to the homely Welsh rabbit or chop and pint of stout in some tavern, has met with the greatest favour from man. But therein lies its weak point. It is essentially a meal for man and not for woman, and there are doubtless many who are not sorry that modern customs are gradually thrusting it out of the list of recognised meals, although it still has, and we believe always will have, enthusiastic devotees. As we have postponed our dinner time from hour to hour, the natural effect has been that the custom of supping has declined. To use a military phrase, the dinner has outflanked it, and it has had to beat a retreat, but in making this flanking movement we have so weakened the centre of our line, that it has been necessary to fill the gap with fresh forces, so, as shown in our engraving, we have called upon our reserves in the shape of that afternoon tea which goes by the name of "a kettledrum," and in this both ladies and gentlemen can mingle, and if it has not the full Bohemian flavour of the supper, that bouquet of jollity which choice spirits love, it is decidedly more refined and elegant. Tea is a beverage which some profess to despise, but hard-workers know its fine qualities and turn not up their noses at the unassuming cup. "Tea in the arbour," which used to be reckoned among the vulgarities of life, has got into society, and in this fine weather, when the sun is shining and the sky is blue and the grass is green, it is much better to talk scandal in the garden than over the tea-table in doors.

In 1882, Mrs. Cecil Hall, an Englishwoman (one gathers of considerable "breeding"), visited her brother on a farm in Manitoba and described the heartiness of the provender:

...Our food is very good and we have the best of all receipts, ravenous appetites for every meal. Our breakfast consists of porridge, bacon and any cold meat, jam, and any quantity of excellent butter and bread. Dinner, a hot joint and a pudding of some sort, finishing up with coffee. Supper, much the same. We have coffee for every meal, and, as the pot is always on the hob, anybody can have a cup when they like. The men have about two cups apiece before breakfast when they first get up. We never mind any amount of coffee, but wage war against the cocktails, taken before meals as appetisers. A cocktail is a horrid concoction of whisky, bitters, sugar and water, which are all mixed together with a "swidel" stick, which stick is always on the wander and for which a search has to be made . . .

HOW TO
DRY PUMPKIN
AND MAKE
PUMPKIN PIE

Cut up your pumpkins and stew them until they are soft and dry. Pound and strain through a colander. Then grease pie pans and spread on the pumpkin ¼ inch thick and dry it. Roll it up and put away in a tight box or bag from insects. Each one of these rolls will make a pie. To make a pumpkin pie soak the roll in sweet milk for 2 hrs., add **1 egg, 1 tbsp. sugar, 1 tsp. ginger** and **1 tsp. allspice**. Bake. If you are lovers of pumpkin pie as we are you will pronounce it good.

~ The Canadian Economist, Ottawa, 1881

Authors' note: It's much easier to use **canned pumpkin** today: **1¾ cups** to **⅔ cup brown sugar** and **1¾ cups canned milk**. Also **¼ cup brandy** helps.

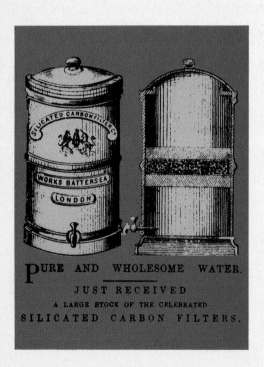

P URE AND WHOLESOME WATER.

JUST RECEIVED
A LARGE STOCK OF THE CELEBRATED
SILICATED CARBON FILTERS.

At Kyuquot in B.C., a missionary, the Rev. Joseph Nicolaye, described an Indian Christmas meal in 1884:

After a general church attendance of the few Indians about, the natives relished a Christmas dinner of a bale of rice and a bucket of molasses. Mr. Campbell and myself found it quite a delicacy to have a slice of bacon.

A schoolteacher named E. A. Howes, who was raised near Glengarry on the St. Lawrence River, Ontario, in the 1880s published, at the end of his life, the following description of a sugar social in his boyhood years:

The house would be crowded, but "the more the merrier." Milk pans, dish pans, pans of all description, as long as they were big enough, were packed with snow. A large boiler filled with syrup or broken sugar was placed on the stove and carefully tended. When the contents of the boiler had reached the required consistency, which could be decided after repeated tasting, quantities were ladled out upon the snow, where it congealed into the finest confection man has ever encountered here below. The paying guests were armed with a table fork and given the personal responsibility of seeing that they secured the worth of their money. There was nothing particularly refined about the whole affair, but there was a happy lack of constraint; since no authority had ever dared to lay down rules of etiquette for such a function there were no rules to be broken. The only restriction was individual capacity, and this was a matter only of private concern; each was master of his own fate and did not worry about it. The Sugar Social was always popular and profitable. . . .

In 1887, Lady Dufferin went camping near the Lake of the Woods with her husband. Since he was, after all, the governor-general, they dined remarkably well:

We had a dinner of hot soup, curry, stewed beef, duck and prairie chicken, and a blueberry pudding, our cook having got up early to pick the blueberries. The soup and the beef were carried here in tins, the game has been shot on the way. Monsieur Beselin, our cook, has done so well. When we were driving he used to arrive sometimes long after us, when it was quite dark, and in five minutes' time he would be hard at work, and our dinner well under way. Mr. McKay, who is a great traveller, said he never saw a man who could produce a dinner so expeditiously, and get his things packed up again so quickly. In addition to this, he is always in a good humour, and in the daytime now he paddles away with a beaming countenance.

Strange to say, though on the banks of a splendid river, we have no good drinking-water, and are obliged to suck it through a sort of baby's bottle filter! In the matter of drink we are badly off; we have brought no wine so as to lessen our luggage; we have no milk (except preserved milk), and, as I said before, good water is hard to get. Tea is our principal beverage, but without milk it is not very nice. We also have chocolate (which makes us thirsty).

In the years immediately preceding the turn of the century Neil MacNeil lived with his grandfather in the farming community of Washabuckt in the heart of Cape Breton Island. He was, many decades later, to describe the wealth of natural produce available for the table:

Nature was generous in producing food in Washabuckt, as it is in most places, providing that man is willing to co-operate with it. The farm animals supplied milk and butter, poultry and eggs, beef and veal, pork and mutton, the field crops yielded oats and barley, potatoes and turnips, and the orchards furnished apples and plums. A few farmers also sowed and reaped wheat and buckwheat. Other popular temperate-zone crops like cabbage and beets, parsnips and carrots, peas and lettuce, were not known or at least they were not grown. Washabuckt was too far north and the growing season was too short for others, like corn, grapes and pears. But the lake teemed with salmon and trout, eels and cod, herring and perch, lobster and oysters, clams and mussels. The forests, too, made their contribution with nuts and maple sugar. Every pasture, in fact every hillside in the open and clearing in the woods, produced a wide variety of luscious wild strawberries, raspberries, blueberries, blackberries and mushrooms. The berries could be enjoyed fresh or they could be preserved for the winter. Finally, there was good hunting and the man of the house could come back with ducks or geese, rabbits or partridge. Thus food was not only abundant, but in wide variety for those who would help themselves to it. The energetic and industrious family could serve a good table. There were those who did not; but it was their own fault.

The storing of food in the home and the barns for the family and the farm stock started early in the spring and continued until late fall. Three or four or more barrels of herring would be salted away in the spring. Large quantities of cod would be salted first and later dried in the sun. During the summer salmon, trout, cod and eels would go fresh to Washabuckt tables, and a calf or two and a lamb or two would be butchered for fresh meat. During the winter eels and smelts would be speared. And the snaring of rabbits and the shooting of ducks and partridge would provide both sport and tasty delicacies.

In 1888, Conyngham Crawford Taylor of Her Majesty's Customs Service looked back over forty years in Toronto and boasted that "as to food, in no city or country can be found more ample or abundant supplies to suit the circumstances of rich or poor":

The display of meats in our markets will compare with the best in Great Britain, comprising even what may be considered delicacies, as venison, and at certain times a "bear steak" is easily procurable.

The fish markets are supplied daily, in addition to those indigenous to our own lakes and rivers, in the shape of salmon, trout, whitefish, muskelonge, and brook trout, with salmon from both the Atlantic and Pacific Oceans, and also from the Saguenay. Cod, haddock, halibut, mackerel, herring, bass, and many other varieties are to be had in abundance. Oysters, in the season, and turtle, of which London aldermen might feel proud, are always within reach. Fowl are so cheap that no family need go without a Christmas goose or turkey, while fruit and vegetables in every variety are plentiful and cheap.

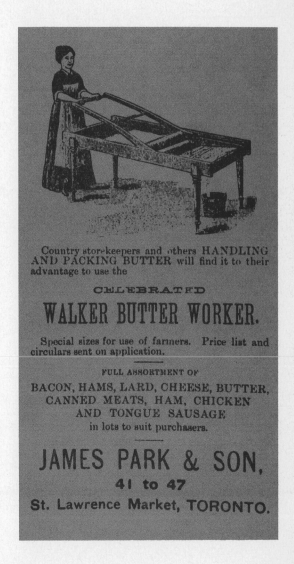
BREAKFAST KEDGEREE

Take some rice which has been boiled the previous day, put it in a saucepan with a little butter to warm over the fire; keep stirring or it will burn. While stirring add left over meat or any cold fish and three or four eggs which have been previously hard boiled and chopped. Continue stirring, seasoning to taste with salt and pepper. When thoroughly hot it should be served immediately, piled high in the centre of a dish on a folded napkin.

~ The Ladies' Journal, Sept. 1884

BUBBLE
AND
SQUEAK

Any remains of **salt pork** or **beef** may be dressed in this good old economical fashion. Cut your meat, when cold, in thin slices, to the weight of about 1 lb. including, if possible, from 2 to 3 oz. of fat; then take **2 or 3 Savoy cabbages**, according to size, which when boiled and chopped ought to weigh about 2 lbs. Cut each cabbage into 4, throw away the outside leaves. Put **1 gal. water** in an iron saucepan. When boiling add your cabbage and let it remain until tender. Drain well and chop fine. Then add **3 oz. butter** in the frying pan, which put on the fire; when hot, put in your slices of meat, which semi-fry of a nice brownish colour on both sides. Take them out, put them on a dish and keep them warm. Then put the cabbage in the pan with the fat, add **1 tsp. salt** and **1 tsp. pepper.**

Stir till hot thoroughly. Put on the dish, lay the meat over and serve. If no cabbage, any greens will do, first boiled, drained, chopped and fried. Boiled carrots and turnips, previously cooked and chopped, may be added to the cabbage.

~ The Canadian Housewife's Manual of Cookery, Hamilton, 1861

Authors' note: Methods of cooking vegetables have improved. Today we use a minimum amount of water to conserve the vitamins. Use only enough water to keep from burning.

SWEETBREADS,
SPANISH SAUCE

Drain and blanch your **sweetbreads** and let them cool. Lard them, line a baking dish with slices of **veal** and **bacon,** and pieces of **onion** and **carrot,** lay the sweetbreads on this, without pressing them, and moisten with stock and **one cup white wine.** Cover with buttered paper and bake for 20 minutes at 400°. When cooked, remove the sweetbreads, put the dressings in another saucepan, and reduce to a glaze. Replace the sweetbreads and reduce again. When browned place the sweetbreads in a serving dish. Loose the glaze from the saucepan by adding a little browning, which you must thin with some stock and pour the resultant sauce over the sweetbreads.

~ Adapted from The Ladies' Journal, 1884

J. V. McAree, for more than half a century the distinguished columnist of the Toronto Globe, recalled towards the end of his life how goods were sold in his family's store in the Cabbagetown area of Toronto:

Not only did the store not advertise, but most of the goods we sold were never advertised. We bought our tea in bulk, our coffee in the bean, and most of the other staples came to us without any trade name to distinguish them from others, any more than if they had been potatoes. But a change was taking place before we left the store. Things were being packaged. Creamery butter had come in, and the first I remember was that of the Locust Hill Farm. It was a novelty. . . .

In the tub-butter days there was a useful implement which I suppose most of my readers have seen. It was called the tester or tryer and was in the form of a long narrow metal cylinder, cut in half lengthwise. This was plunged into the tub of butter, penetrating for a distance of several inches. Then, it was given a quick half turn and the core of butter could be withdrawn. The expert would run his nose along the butter, and perhaps taste a bit here and there to make sure that the butter was all of the same even quality from top to bottom. This fact ascertained, the tryer would be reinserted in the hole and the core returned to its original position.

Before the packaging of tea was invented to make the fortunes of Lipton, Larkin and a host of others, the grocers bought tea in large chests, weighing perhaps fifty pounds or more. They were lined with lead foil, and the outside was formed of a thin layer of wood. It was one of the arts of the grocer to blend the tea he retailed from two or three different chests. . . .

Another commodity whose price did not vary, if I am to trust my memory, was coffee. We sold it for 40 cents a pound, two of the ounces being composed of chicory. There was no deception here. Everybody knew chicory had been added, and everybody was glad that it should be so for the chicory was supposed to add desired body. We had a small coffee mill in the store and here the coffee was ground fresh.

Indian Black Teas.

Vol. XIV.—No. 22.   MONTREAL, SATURDAY, DECEMBER 9, 1876.   { SINGLE COPIES, TEN CENTS.
                                                                 { $4 PER YEAR IN ADVANCE.

SUGAR: GONE UP, OUT OF SIGHT.—(Market Reports, November, 1876.)

CUSTOMER :—Them's free-trade prices to consumers, be they ? Then protect Home Manufactures to death, sez I. I'd a'taken two pounds
refined at the old Redpath price.   Gi'me a quarter pound brown ; that'll have to do for a week, *now.*

GROCER :—Very sorry, Ma'am, but we are positively losing money on sugar, even at these prices.   (More's the pity. *Ed. note.*)

THRee HAbiTAnT dishes

When Upper Canadians were subsisting on greasy pork slabs and mushy beans, the French Canadians, using much the same ingredients, were enjoying traditional dishes like these. Prepared by chef Jean Guay at *Le Fournil* in the Bonsecours area of Montreal, they differ only a little from the kind of food that habitants were serving at the time of Confederation.

LA TRUITE

Take a rainbow trout of one pound or more, salt inside and out and place on a large plate. Squeeze the juice of 2 *lemons* over it, add a glass of *Jamaica rum* and put in refrigerator to marinate for one hour. Then wrap the fish tightly in a sheet of aluminum foil and bake in a 500° oven for at least 30 minutes. Unwrap the trout, place on a platter, cut it in half lengthwise, remove the bones and garnish with lemon circles, boiled potatoes and round beets.

FEVES AU LARD CANADIENNES

Soak *1 lb. white or yellow beans* at least 12 hours in water. Save the fluid, remove and rinse the beans and cook for 30 minutes or until tender. Mix *½ tsp. dry mustard, ¼ tsp. black pepper, 1 tsp. salt* with *½ cup of molasses*. Fill cup with water. Put beans in a casserole and cover with ingredients in cup adding fluid from soaking until beans are covered. Place *½ lb. salt pork* in boiling water for five minutes. Remove and clean. Cut in half-inch cubes and add it to the beans together with *3 onions*, chopped fine. Cover casserole and cook in a 250° oven for seven or eight hours adding water every two hours if necessary. Two hours before serving remove cover so beans will brown.

TOURTIERE

Put the following ingredients into a pot: *1 lb. chopped pork; 1 small diced onion; 1 garlic bud; ½ tsp. salt; ½ tsp. savory; ¼ tsp. celery pepper; ¼ tsp. cloves* and *½ cup water*. Bring to a boil, cook for 20 minutes, remove from fire. Slowly add *½ cup bread crumbs*, spoonful by spoonful, pausing at intervals, until all fat has disappeared from the top. Allow mixture to cool, pour into a pie shell, cover with more crust and cook for 25 minutes or until crust is golden in a 500° oven.

2/Dining Out in the Good Old Days

The Dining Room of the Russell House, Ottawa, 1873, at dinner time.
A contemporary engraving.

The breakfast menu of the famous Queen's Hotel in Toronto, *circa* 1887, is a gustatory delight. The mouth salivates, the taste buds tingle, and the very senses reel at the variety – nay, the vastness of it. Those were the days when breakfast was an event, not an interlude. A man's girth was the measure of his social stature and the idea of a couple of soft-boiled eggs gulped from a glass or a Danish and coffee gobbled on the gallop would have offended the propriety of those times when eating was a ritual and breakfast a sacrament.

There are forty-three fish, meat and egg dishes on this menu, not to mention *ten varieties of bread* plus fruit, marmalade and beverages. And, in the words of one astonished British traveller, "you are at liberty to partake of all of them if you like and are

young enough to do so." You could at one sitting knock off a salt codfish in cream, a dozen oysters on the half shell, a plate of tripe and onions, another of pickled pig's feet, a side dish of stewed potatoes, a ham omelet, a stack of griddle cakes with maple syrup and a flagon of green tea – and many did just that. The price? Why, the price was included, because the hotel, like all the great hotels of those days, was on the American plan. You paid $2.50 for your bed, your breakfast and two other meals even more gargantuan. "The man of thrift," we are told, "usually attends them all."

Not all the inns and restaurants across the new nation served food in the grand manner of the Queen's and the other great mid-Victorian hostelries. *Ixion,* a commentator in the *Canadian Illus-*

trated News of 1873, decried the fare to be found in so many station restaurants in the new Confederation when he attacked "the gutta percha steaks, the greasy chops, the flabby sections of sickly looking fish, the bean-flour coffee and the currant-leaf tea, which are served as refreshments by the keepers of the wayside eating places along our iron roads."

In the unsettled west, where hotels were often little more than clapboard or log shanties and where guests shared rooms and even beds with strangers, public eating left a good deal to be desired. Shortly after the Canadian Pacific Railway was built, Edward Roper, a perceptive if somewhat class-conscious English traveller, praised the Colonial Hotel in New Westminster, B.C., because "there were actually handles to the tea cups which struck us as a great improvement on Vancouver style" and because "here, too, there was a steak that could be eaten."

Roper took a dim view of most Canadian hotels, save those that were being constructed by the new railway company: "Their hotels are far and away the best that I have ever stayed in in America." The rest, he felt, put quantity before quality: It was all very well for Canadians to "brag about their immense dining rooms, to expatiate on their amazingly comprehensive bills of fare when it is next to impossible to get a slice of properly cooked meat . . . or to be served even in a manner that a second-rate middle-class home would be in Britain."

But the chief complaint that most travellers had in Canada was that meals were available only at specific hours. One wrote ruefully of the Queen's that "if you happen to arrive at the hotel late at night or between any of the fixed meal times you can get nothing to eat until the next one comes around, which is distressing to the last degree." Annie Brassey, later a baroness, wrote of Niagara Falls' famous Clifton House in 1872 that "everyone is obliged to breakfast before ten, dine between three and four, and have tea at eight whether they like it or not, nothing whatsoever is to be had afterward or at any other time than these specified hours." Roper, checking into Glacier House in the Selkirk Mountains of British Columbia at midnight, went to bed supperless, asking: "When will those who are supposed to provide for the comfort of their guests remember that there are certain circumstances under which 'something to eat' is a necessity at other times than at regular meal hours? But in public places and in private, too, often and often, such a want is looked upon as an absurd and almost unnatural desire."

A glance at Edwin C. Guillet's monumental *Pioneer Inns and Taverns* shows how ubiquitous the wayside hostelries were. They were the motels of their day, boasting "good stabling and attentive ostlers always in attendance." But of the grand hotels of eastern Canada four deserve specific mention: the Queen's in Toronto, whose breakfasts have already been described (the town's leading hotel from 1862 to the turn of the century, it stood on the site of the present Royal York); the Rossin House, also in Toronto; the St. Lawrence Hall in Montreal; and the St. Louis Hotel in Quebec City.

At the time of Confederation, you could stay at the St. Louis for fourteen shillings a day, American plan. At breakfast and lunch there were at least twenty dishes to choose from; at dinner, at least forty "and the opportunity of eating of each, with dessert afterwards." The hotel held four or five hundred guests, most of whom, unable to squeeze into the public sitting room, crowded the corridors. Informed that the establishment lacked a dinner bell, Lady Duffus Hardy inquired of an Irish chambermaid how she would know when meals were served. "Oh, ye'll know," cried the girl. " 'E 'ollers!" When the hollering began, guests of all nationalities thundered into the dining hall, bolting their food with gusto – "some almost the entire bill of fare." And no wonder; for, according to David Kennedy, a member of a family of Scottish vocalists who had travelled across most of the Empire, the St. Louis set the best table he had encountered in four years of travel. Lady Duffus Hardy recalled seeing one man "who handled his eating utensils with such marvellous dexterity that when his knife flashed into the air and disappeared down his throat, I watched for it to come out of the back of his head."

The St. Lawrence Hall in Montreal was the first in Canada to occupy a full city block. George Tuthill Borrett, a fellow of King's College, Cambridge, stayed there in 1864 and described it in enthusiastic detail: "I must ask you to imagine a fine handsome house after the style of the new hotels in London with a noble entrance hall fronted by a covered arcade opening upon a wide, well-built street . . ." The dining hall was "an elegant room . . . entered by splendidly wide passages or corridors and filled with innumerable small tables." Again, "breakfast was the most striking meal" and you were expected to eat heartily. Anyone who ordered a single dish was virtually ignored by the waiters: "A man who sits down and orders an egg and a bit of toast has just as much chance of getting anyone to wait upon him as he has of seeing the Thames pure or the Conservatives in office."

These great dining halls were all cyclopean. In its heyday the Rossin House in Toronto was considered to be the best hotel west of New York. Its original dining room was one hundred feet long by almost forty feet wide, with an eighteen-foot ceiling. But it was only part of a veritable labyrinth of ancillary chambers. Adjoining it was a carving room, a dish room, a dessert room and a glazing gallery, connected to kitchen and china pantry. The hotel began as a coffee house in 1832 and was rebuilt after the great Toronto fire of 1862. It played host to most of the notables who visited the new Dominion, from Edward Prince of Wales to the great Lily Langtry. At the time of Confederation you could stay there for $2.50, including, of course, three whopping meals. You can still stay there, for the hotel continues to operate as the Prince George. But $2.50 today will scarcely pay for one of those two-egg breakfasts with toast that the waiters of that flamboyant era ignored so studiously. And where, at any hotel in the land, can you today get codfish in cream, tripe and onions, and pickled pig's feet, all at one sitting, be it breakfast, luncheon, dinner or high tea? Those days belong to the past.

DIDN'T RECOGNIZE THE BIVALVES

MR. BYAM KEGGS (from Kalamazoo, with intense disgust) – *Here, waiter, I ordered raw oysters. What on airth are these nasty black stones?*

WAITER (petrified) – *Oystahs, sah—on de haff-shell, sah!*

MR. BYAM KEGGS – *Half-shell, is it? Oh, git out! I've eat a million canned oysters out home and never was a shell on ary one of them!—Puck.*

FRICANDEAU

Chop fine **3½ lbs. cold roast veal** and mix with it **1 tbsp. salt**, **1 tbsp. pepper**, **¼ tsp. nutmeg**, **1 crumbled cracker** and **3 eggs**. If the veal is thin (lean) add a piece of **butter** half as large as an egg and **1 tbsp. cream**. Form all this in a large roll and spot the roll over with bits of butter; then strew over it more cracker crumbs. Bake slowly for 2 hours, adding a little water from time to time. Chill and slice thinly.

~ The Home Cook Book, Toronto, 1877

Anthony Trollope, the distinguished English novelist, was also an inveterate writer of travel books – as were so many Victorian men of letters. Shortly before 1862 he visited Canada and later published this amusing account of his experiences in a wayside inn at Sherbrooke, Quebec:

I have said that the Canadians hereabouts are somewhat slow. As we were driving back to Sherbrooke it became necessary that we should rest for an hour or so in the middle of the day, and for this purpose we stopped at a village inn. It was a large house, in which there appeared to be three public sitting-rooms of ample size, one of which was occupied as the bar. In this there were congregated some six or seven men seated in arm-chairs round a stove, and among these I placed myself. No one spoke a word either to me or to any one else. No one smoked, and no one read, nor did they even whittle sticks. I asked a question first of one and then of another, and was answered with monosyllables. So I gave up any hope in that direction, and sat staring at the big stove in the middle of the room, as the others did. Presently another stranger entered, having arrived in a waggon as I had done. He entered the room and sat down, addressing no one, and addressed by none. After a while, however, he spoke. "Will there be any chance of dinner here?" he said. "I guess there'll be dinner by-and-by," answered the landlord, and then there was silence for another ten minutes, during which the stranger stared at the stove. "Is that dinner any way ready?" he asked again. "I guess it is," said the landlord. And then the stranger went out

30

to see after his dinner himself. When we started at the end of an hour nobody said anything to us. The driver "hitched" on the horses, as they call it, and we started on our way, having been charged nothing for our accommodation.

Viscount Milton and his doctor friend, Cheadle, left this rather rueful description of hotel life in the Cariboo district of British Columbia in 1863 at the height of the gold rush:

Our quarters at Cusheon's Hotel were vile. A blanket spread on the floor of a loft was our bedroom, but the swarms of lice which infested the place rendered sleep almost impossible, and made us think with regret on the soft turf of the prairie, or a mossy couch in the woods. The fare, limited to beefsteaks, bread and dried apples, was wretchedly cooked and frightfully expensive. Beef was worth fifty cents or two shillings a pound, flour the same, a "drink" of anything except water was half a dollar, nor could the smallest article, even a box of matches, be bought for less than a "quarter" – one shilling. Before we reached Williams Creek we paid a dollar and a quarter, or five shillings, for a single pint bottle of stout.

The scholarly Englishman, George Tuthill Borrett, staying at Montreal's St. Lawrence Hall in 1864, discovered that the way to impress a waiter was to pretend to order almost everything – even if you didn't want it. Here is his description of his first breakfast:

I found myself in about two minutes surrounded by a multitude of little oval dishes, on which were fish, steaks, chops, ham, chicken, turkey, rissoles, potatoes (boiled, roast and fried), cabbage, corn, cheese, onions and pickles, besides plates of hot rolls, buns, crumpets, toast and biscuits, flanked by a great jug full of milk and an enormous vessel of coffee. However, in the midst of my bewilderment, which seemed to puzzle the waiter, who had taken my order as a thing of every day occurrence, my friend the banker turned up, and with his help I succeeded in demolishing a considerable portion of the formidable array of dishes. But there was a Yankee next to us who ordered much the same as I had thus unintentionally been burdened with, and what was our astonishment to see him take *six* soft-boiled eggs, and breaking them on the edge of a tumbler, drop in successively their respective yolks, and then, after two or three whirls of his spoon in the glass, gobble them up as an "appetiser," with a gurgle of delight that was quite musical. This was only the preliminary canter. You might have thought perhaps, that at any rate he was off on his raid upon the menu, but no, he was only going through his paces previous to entering upon the severer work before him, and when he *did* set to, "my eye, warn't it a caution to snakes?" Fish, steaks, chops, sausages, omelets, with vegetables of several kinds, vanished like gnats before a thunderstorm; coffee and tea chased one another down that capacious throat, till, in less than three quarters of an hour from the firing of the first shot, the table was well nigh cleared, and a glass of iced milk brought to a triumphant close this interesting performance.

St. Lawrence Hall, Montreal, by C. W. Jefferys

Luncheon is served on the same liberal scale, dinner, tea, and supper, ditto. It is no use trying to shirk a dish, the waiters will insist on your trying everything, so your only course is to try. Everybody tries every dish; no one feels any compunction at leaving untouched what has been brought to him; waste is immaterial, for meat is dirt-cheap, vegetables and fruit abundant. All ages of either sex eat extravagantly; no one looks astonished to see "a lovely plant of sixteen summers," tucking down at breakfast kidneys, ham, and sausages after a tremendous plateful of fish; no one stares to see a precocious youth of nine going straight through the dinner carts like a steam mowing-machine, puffing, and blowing, and spitting like an ill-used engine. It is a wonderful thing, truly, this Yankee appetite.

John J. Rowan, an English "emigrant and sportsman," visited Canada in 1875 to give advice to "people of small fortune whose means though ample to enable them to live in Canada are insufficient to meet the demands of rising expenses at home." He thought Canadian hotels very fair and the charges reasonable enough, "but one gets tired of the crowd, the racket and the din."

The ordinary crowd in the dining room of a large Canadian hotel is an interesting study. There are the commercial travellers who do congregate together, and are charged at lower rates than the ordinary travelling public, as are also the residents, who are boarded by the week or the month at less than half the rates charged to tourists. Uncle Sam is sure to be there with his wife and daughters, who dress to astonish the natives, and succeed. There is the travelling theatrical or operatic troupe, the members of which are contracted for at so much a head; the temperance men, who make up for no drinking by eating enormously, and who get a little surreptitious stimulant out of the pudding sauce, which the cook, who knows their tastes, furnishes in gallons; the burly senator from the country, who carries his senatorial labours lightly; the MPs *and* MPPs, who, perhaps, enjoy themselves all the more as their grateful country pays the bill; the judge on circuit; the militia colonel on his rounds, and the English tourist and his wife; the former is strictly on the defensive, and the latter shows her sovereign contempt for the smartness of the ladies by her austere simplicity of costume; and last, but not least, there are the inevitable bride and bridegroom. These unfortunate persons have always the knack of blundering or simpering into the great dining hall in such a way as to attract as much attention as possible.

As for the dinners, they are generally very good, but barbarously put on the table. Although Canadian hotels have made a great stride in civilization – I mean late dinners – the art of dining in these places is still in its infancy. What can a man possibly do with a dozen different dishes all at once before him? This style of living suits the Yankees, I believe, but Canadians ought to manage these things better in their hotels. On one occasion I sat next to a lady from Vermont who fed promiscuously off nine dishes, viz. one fish, three entremets, two rots, three vegetables; she then topped off with pudding, cheese, and a cup of tea, and the whole meal from first to last only occupied twelve minutes by my watch. This hasty feeding would kill an Englishman; it does make the Yankee bilious, but it seems to have no bad effect on the Canadian traveller.

The Queen's Hotel, Toronto

LOBSTERS POTTED
AS AT
QUEEN'S HOTEL

Take out the meat of **1 lobster**, as whole as you can; split the tail and remove the gut; if the inside be not watery, add that. Season with a dash each of **mace, nutmeg, white pepper, salt** and **powdered clove**. Lay a little fine **butter** at the bottom of a pan and the lobster smooth over it, with **bay leaves** between. Cover it with butter and bake gently. When done, pour the whole on the bottom of a sieve and with a fork lay the pieces into potting pots, some of each sort, with the seasoning above it. When cold, pour clarified butter over, but not hot. It will be good next day; or, if highly seasoned and thick covered with butter, will keep some time. Potted lobster may be used cold or as a fricassee with cream sauce; and then it looks very nicely, and eats excellently, especially if there is spawn.

~ Mrs. Clarke's Cookery Book, Toronto, 1883

In the same year, David Kennedy Jr., the travelling Scottish vocalist, back from four years' tour of Australia, New Zealand, and other bastions of Empire, described his visit that June to the only hotel in St. John's, Newfoundland – "a small house with accommodation for about fourteen people":

The boarders, who were chiefly Montreal and Halifax business men, sat together at one table, the head of which was graced by our landlord and his lady, in the ancient hostelry fashion. It resembled a family party more than a *table d'hote* – all conversation was in common and the joke and laugh went freely round. The fare was capital, and of course largely composed of fish. We had cod every day for dinner, save when a splendid salmon burst upon us – its plump, aristocratic form reposing in a tin dish about three feet long. Once indeed, we had fried "caplin," but they could not hold a candle to sprats as regards flavour. A plate of fishes' tongues, too, was placed on the table one day, but proved rather a failure. "A cod, a cod; the whole edible kingdom for a cod!" We never tired of cod, boiled or fried – it was a princely dish. Even the salmon, caught outside the Heads, and as large in size as it was delicate in flavour and free from heavy oiliness, was not to be compared to the cod. It would almost be worth living in Newfoundland for this alone. Our taste was also gratified in the matter of vegetables, which were cooked in the Irish fashion – boiled, that is, along with pork or ham. Occasionally, too, in default of cabbage, we had dandelions and turnip-tops – "neep-shaws" being accounted as much of a luxury here as in Cockneydom.

In 1878 and again in 1881, The Times of London sent its widely travelled correspondent, W. Fraser Rae, to Canada. He had a thoroughly enjoyable time (weeds and flowers especially fascinated him) though he felt that Canada's ultimate fate was to be swallowed by the U.S. Here is his description of life in prairie hotels. The Pacific, mentioned below, was in Winnipeg:

The emigrant or traveller who is prepared to camp out will find life on the prairie far less unbearable than if he depend for shelter at night in a settler's hut. It is trying to toil along the miry paths over which thirty miles are all that can be conveniently passed between sunrise and sunset, but the accommodation at the few stopping-places on the beaten track is quite as great a trial to the fastidious wayfarers. These prairie hotels are the rude loghouses erected by settlers who add to their incomes by entertaining travellers. They are commonly eighteen feet long by sixteen feet wide and are divided horizontally into two parts. On the ground floor is the place where the family and the visitors sit and take the meals which are cooked in a stove at the one end, the stove serving the double purpose of heating the house and affording the requisite facilities for cooking. In the upper storey the occupants of the house pass the night. The food is plain and simple enough to satisfy the greatest foe to high living, consisting of fried salt pork, bread, potatoes and tea. Eggs and milk are luxuries rarely obtainable. Why the settlers do not rear poultry or keep cows is a question which I cannot answer.

One of the fish on the bill of fare at the Pacific Hotel bore the name of Red River salmon. I tasted it and thought it delicious, though not at all like any salmon which I had eaten. It was quite as rich as salmon

THE OLD CURRANT SAUCE FOR VENISON

Boil **1 oz. dried currants** in **½ pint water** for **5** minutes. Add **½ cup bread crumbs**, **6 cloves**, **1 glass port wine** and **1 tsp. butter.** Stir until smooth, remove from heat and pour over venison.

~ The Canadian Housewife's Manual of Cookery, Hamilton, Ontario, 1861

LORD CLIVE'S CURRY

Slice **6 onions** and **1 green apple**. Stew in **2 cups beef stock** to which **1 clove garlic**, minced, has been added, until ingredients are reduced to a pulp. Add **1 tsp. curry powder**, **¼ cup beef stock**, **1 tsp. salt**, **½ tsp. cayenne**, **½ tsp. black pepper.** Cut up into small cubes **1lb. chicken, veal, lamb** or **beef** and add to the gravy together with a walnut-sized piece of **butter** rolled in **flour.** Stew slowly for **2½ hours.**

~ Warwick's Everyday Cookery, Toronto, circa 1870

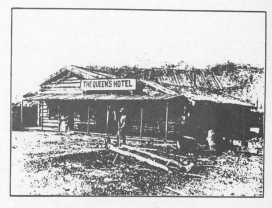

The Queen's Hotel, Golden, B.C., circa 1887

Recipes from The Canadian Economist, compiled by the Ladies Association of Bank St. Church, Ottawa, 1881

FRIED FINGERS

Cut stale bread in slices, rather thick. Cut these in fingers. Prepare a custard by beating an egg, adding milk, sugar and flavouring. In this soak the bread for 1 hour or more. Fry these in butter and arrange on a dish in the form of a pyramid. Sprinkle with sugar and put jelly around.

SORREL SOUP

This is a most wholesome soup, which would be most popular in America if it were better known. For four quarts of soup: Put into a saucepan a piece of **butter**, the size of an egg, **3 sprigs parsley, 3 leaves lettuce, 1 onion** and **1 pint sorrel**,—all finely chopped. Add **nutmeg, pepper** and **salt** to taste, cover and let them cook or sweat 10 minutes. Then add **2 tsps. flour**, mix well, and gradually add **3 qts. boiling beef stock.** Beat the **yolks of 4 eggs** and mix them with **1 cup cream.** Add **1 tsp. chervil** to the soup, let it boil 10 minutes, then stir in the eggs and cream and serve hot (or cold).

CHARCOAL GINGER CAKE

Mix together **½ cup butter, ½ cup molasses, 1 cup brown sugar, ½ cup water, ½ tsp. ginger, ½ tsp. soda, 2 tsps. pulverized charcoal** and **flour** enough to roll. Cut into shape with a cake cutter and bake on a greased cookie sheet at 350° for 8 minutes.

and had scarcely any bones, resembling a lamprey in this respect more closely than any fish with which I am acquainted. A travelling-companion was quite as much pleased with it as I was. Before eating and praising it, he had warned me against ever eating catfish, which he had seen taken out of the river, and of which he disliked the look as well as the name. He was rather surprised to learn that he had heartily enjoyed and commended catfish under the name of Red River salmon.

In 1882, Mrs. Cecil Hall, visiting her brother on a Manitoba farm, left this brief description of prairie inns for her genteel English readers:

The food provided at these wayside inns is generally so bad and dear, a dollar a head charged for sixteen-eighteen dishes of almost uneatable messes, that we prefer the tinned meats and fruits we have in our luncheon basket; and for drinks we have beautifully iced water in all the carriages, the ice being replenished at every big station.

The most flamboyant tavern in Montreal in the 1880s was Joe Beef's Canteen. Edgar Andrew Collard, a long-time student of early Montreal history, described it for his readers, some years ago, in the Montreal Gazette:

When the door swung open into the night, the smell of buffalo would sweep out, hard and unmistakable. There would be a clamour of voices, the flash of light, and a glimpse of a confused and dishevelled crowd.

Once he was inside the door he would have in front of him, as one old account says, "the rarest collection of men his eyes had ever seen. There was not a good coat, or a hat in even moderate repair, in the entire company. Their garb was of the poorest, but it made no difference to their spirits – all hands were happy and contented."

In a corner of the room was a stack of loaves of bread, piled as high as the ceiling. It was a sort of wide-open pantry.

Anyone who wished might help himself, and a crowd was sitting or standing and eating heartily. And, of course, there was Joe Beef's bar.

Joe Beef operated not only a canteen but a menagerie. In the corner opposite the pile of loaves lay a black bear. The rattle of the chain from time to time warned the inquisitive to keep at a distance. The odour of buffalo was meanwhile rising strongly from the cellar. Down the stairs the visitor would be taken.

In a corner of the dark cellar a space had been boarded off. There a buffalo was chained. It was a matter for wonder how the buffalo had been brought into the canteen and down those stairs, but there it was – a rather tamed buffalo but a buffalo nonetheless.

In another part of the cellar was a second bear. Two parrots, almost as devoid of feathers as broiled chicken, swung from a bar near the roof, screeching or chattering. In the farther corner, scarcely lit by the smoky lamp, other forms might be seen stirring. But by this time the visitor, if not seeing as much as he might like, had smelt more than he could stand, and probably retreated up the stairs. . . .

Joe Beef was the chief attraction of his establishment. His Irish

The Ottawa Hotel, 1870

HOTEL KEEPER'S BUTTER

This is very simple and good and will keep potted for a long time. It is excellent with all broiled meats. Put on a plate ¼ lb. fresh butter, ¼ tsp. salt, ¼ tsp. pepper, 2 tsps. chopped parsley, juice of 1 lemon and a **dash nutmeg**. Mix and reform into pats and chill.

~ The Canadian Housewife's Manual of Cookery, Hamilton, Ontario, 1861

The Halifax Hotel, 1889

Joe Beef of Montreal, the *Son* of the People.

He cares not for Pope, Priest, Parson or King William of the Boyne; all Joe wants is the Coin. He **trusts** in God in summer time to keep him from all harm; when he sees the frost and snow poor ol I Joe trusts **to the** Almighty Dollar and good old maple wood to keep his belly warm, for Churches, Chapels, Ranters **Preachers**, Beechers and such stuff Montreal has already got enough.

FROM THE ' EVENING STAR," APRIL 15, 1876.

Mr. John Dougall in the *New York Witness*, makes an appeal for " additional capital to the extent of fifty thousand dollars." He proposes to issue bonds of $10, $50, $100 and $500, payable in five years, and bearing 7 per cent. interest.

JOE BEEF.

Any citizens, this day, having any of their Bonds on Hand, will please call at my Office from 10 a.m. to 12 a.m. daily, or at next door, the Rag Store, and they will get their full value, as far as old paper goes !

All you Clergymen, Captains, Sailors, Bums, and Scurvy-Tailors, if you can walk or crawl, when you go on the spree, go and see JOE BEEF of Montreal.

The Village Magistrate.

The City Councillor.

The Sunday School Bouncer.

The Blooming Rose with the Temperance Nose.

All you Clergymen, Captains, Sailors, Bums and Scurvy-Tailors, if you can walk or crawl, when you go on the spree, go and see JOE BEEF of Montreal.

wit, ready and provocative, kept him famous. He was a versatile rhymester, and one of his long and impudent rhymes is carved on his tombstone. His humour even marked the day of his wife's funeral.

She predeceased him some time in the early 1880s, and was buried in Mount Royal Cemetery. Joe, who still retained a commissary function in the militia, had the regimental band at the funeral. On the way up to the cemetery, the band played the *Dead March* from *Saul*. On the way back, so it is said, it struck up, at Joe's request, the old army tune, *The Girl I Left Behind Me*.

Stuart Cumberland, FRGS, was commissioned by a syndicate of Australian, Indian and English newspapers to cross Canada by rail as soon as the CPR's last spike was driven. "I am positively the first person to go over the line of rail between the Pacific and the Atlantic in a journalistic sense," he claimed. He was pleasantly surprised at his reception in New Westminster:

The principal hotel in New Westminster is most comfortable, and the table is excellent as well as abundant. Salmon cutlets and sturgeon steaks deliciously cooked, hot rolls with pats of guinea-gold butter, and jugs of fresh, thick cream and well-made tea and coffee graced the breakfast table; and the midday dinner included oyster soup, marrow-bones, roast and boiled joints, and fat tender chicken. The vegetables were a treat in themselves, whilst luscious fruits of various kinds were in abundance at every meal. The charge per day was, I believe, from $1.50 to $2.00, a considerable reduction being allowed permanent boarders. Next to the Driard House at Victoria the hotel at New Westminster was decidedly the best house I "struck" from the Pacific to Manitoba.

That inveterate traveller, Edward Roper, was less enchanted by the breakfast served at Le Grand House in Vancouver or, later in his travels, by Brett's Sanitarium at Banff:

They don't seem to know what a dish-cover is in America; they certainly did not at the Le Grand House. Nor did we ever see a joint there, or at any other hotel. For breakfast fruit is generally eaten first, if there is any on the table; but oatmeal porridge always follows. Then, the attendant having very gently whispered in your ear what is provided, you give your order. A curious thing, I don't remember a waitress in the Great North-West who spoke above a whisper. They evidently thought that speaking out plainly would be rough, or rude; and, mind you, Canadians are great on "tone."

Having made out what it is the girl has said, you give your order. West of Calgary, salmon is sure to be an item, three times a day. You choose, then, salmon, with ham and eggs to follow. In time, not hurriedly, she will come in with a tray, on which will be at least a dozen small oval white pie-dishes, in each of which will be some different food. Salmon in one, which was invariably baked till a crust had formed all around it like a shell, and we had to crack it to get to the edible portion, which, when we reached, it proved so dry and tasteless that it was little wonder we quickly got "so tired of salmon." The fish was good enough when properly cooked, but, at the Le Grand House, they never gave us sauce or trimmings, just the hard baked fish. In another of

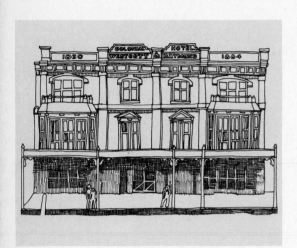

The Colonial Hotel, New Westminster, B.C.

WHITE SOUP

Pound **6 oz. roasted sweet almonds, 6 oz. breast of roasted chicken, 3 oz. white bread** soaked in **veal stock** and squeezed dry. Beat all to a paste and pour over it **2 qts. boiling veal stock.** Strain through a hair sieve and add **1 pint thick cream.** Serve as soon as it reaches the point of boiling.

~ Mrs. Clarke's Cookery Book, Grip Publishing, Toronto, 1883 these small oval dishes would be ham, in another eggs; one would contain a piece of toast, another potatoes in their skins, the next one apple sauce, several with different kinds of bread or buckwheat cakes, molasses in another, or maple syrup, and, perhaps, there will be a slice or two of flat American pie.

This row of little dishes will be placed in a semi-circle round you, with a cup of coffee, strange in flavour. They never use hot milk there, and the cups are without handles, much skill being needed to get one safely to your mouth. They will give you one large plated fork of heavy make, with a metal-handled knife, the blade of which is steel that was once silvered over, but the silver having worn off in patches, and the steel become black and corroded, the result is a very unpleasant implement to eat with, which most people there consider the proper purpose of a knife, as well as to cut with. They never use steel knives unsilvered; to save the trouble of cleaning, doubtless.

The clang of a bell resounding through the house brought us all down to breakfast in the morning. The room was almost in darkness, and we could just see that the cruet-stands were enveloped in gauze, and each sugar-basin covered with a piece of muslin. "Why is this thus," we asked, "and why this dim religious light?" "To keep out flies," was the rejoinder; "besides, it keeps the place cool."

When we got our food we did not rejoice, though we were hungry. The salmon was baked till it rattled on the plate as if it was a bare bone. The steak was dried to the consistency of a chip, ditto the mutton-chop. The English breakfast-bacon was a fraud; one couldn't bite it. The coffee was a delusion, and we always wondered of what rare herb they used to make the "English breakfast tea." But there were plenty of eggs. What a blessing it is they are always plentiful in that glorious land! There was very decent bread, so we did not starve.

Two young Englishmen sitting at our table remarked they supposed we didn't think very much of the food, but added, "If you had been for twelve months in a shanty north of Calgary, and hadn't sat down to a proper meal all that time, you would think this splendid." Perhaps we should.

Douglas Sladen, editor of the British Who's Who, made what he called "a pilgrimage along the Queen's Highway" from Halifax to Victoria towards the end of the century. Here he describes a French-Canadian country inn at Rivière du Loup:

We arrived at Rivière du Loup in time for lunch, which in these primitive parts is a dinner washed down by tea. This was perhaps our first introduction to the Canadian country hotel, where the tables and table-cloths look as if they were one flesh and washed together. They are more attractive to flies than a country grocery; the cruet and the sugar basin never leave the table, relays being added to the top when the flies and dust have been picked over pretty carefully. . . . Tea is included in the price of every meal; consequently very little else is drunk except by the fastidious English globe-trotter. Breakfast is bacon and eggs, dinner is underdone joints, and supper is chops and steaks. Passengers and the train hands sit down together; the former are considered intruders and made to know their place. Dead flies are the least objectionable part of these hotels.

ALMOND SOUP

This is a usual dish for Christmas supper and is eaten hot. It is of almost Arcadian simplicity. Throw some **sweet almonds** in boiling water to get rid of the husks and skins. Pound them in a mortar with some lukewarm water, adding by degrees pounded **white sugar** and pounded **cinnamon.** Turn it out on a plate or dish which must be able to stand the fire, previously lining the bottom with fingers of **bread** powdered with **cinnamon.** Thoroughly heat these ingredients over a clear fire and serve.

~ Mrs. Clarke's Cookery Book, Toronto, 1883

The St. Charles restaurant, 70 Yonge Street, Toronto, 1888

The Dining Car Breakfast

Sir William Van Horne, the construction genius who built and ran the Canadian Pacific, was not only a noted gourmet but also a far-sighted man. From the outset he saw that a railway linking both oceans could expect a fastidious and sophisticated clientele from both Europe and the Orient. Thus did the CPR become noted for the glory of its cuisine – a cuisine that made brilliant use of native Canadian dishes, from Winnipeg goldeye and Lake Superior trout to Oka cheese and maple syrup. To this day the line retains the tradition of the gargantuan Victorian breakfast with which it launched its dining car service in 1886. In such a breakfast the *pièce de résistance* is corned beef hash with an egg on top. The authors are pleased to present their own version below:

CORNED BEEF HASH

Crumble *1 tin bully beef* in a bowl and marinate overnight in red wine. Chop *1 large potato* and *1 large onion* very fine. Mix with corned beef, add *1 egg* and mix again. Add *2 tbsps. red wine* and season with *1 tsp. black pepper*, freshly ground, *2 tsps. celery salt*, *2 tbsps. chopped parsley*, *1 tsp. monosodium glutamate*. Sift in *2 tbsps. pancake flour*. Mix again. Heat an iron skillet with a small amount of bacon fat covering the bottom. Ladle the hash into the pan in pancake-sized patties, formed with a spatula. Cover the uncooked top with dry English mustard, turn and brown. Cover the other side with dry English mustard and turn again. Break 1 raw egg over each cake and allow to cook. When white has turned milky pour *1 tbsp. red wine* on each cake. As soon as wine has penetrated, serve. For 4 persons.

3/Eating on the Move: 1860-1895

DINING CAR

THE CANADIAN PACIFIC RAILWAY

It is an interesting coincidence that the concept of eating on wheels is almost exactly as old as the Canadian nation. And it is significant and proper that it actually had its beginnings in Canada. For it was in June of 1867 on the Great Western Railway of Canada that the Pullman Palace Car company put into service for the first time a new kind of moving hotel. This "hotel car" or "palace car" as it was variously called was a sleeper with a kitchen at one end – the forerunner of the more durable dining car. For the first time meals were served aboard a moving train, at tables placed in the sections. And the meals themselves, considering the cramped quarters, were remarkably varied: The menu for June 1, 1867, lists oysters – fried, roasted or raw – a variety of cold meats and salads, three kinds of roast meats, half a dozen egg dishes, including a rum omelet, and French drip coffee.

When the Grand Trunk introduced one of these new cars in 1870, *The Canadian Illustrated News* was lavish in its reportage:

"It was the object of much interest and unbounded admiration to all who had the opportunity of seeing it. For elegance and beauty it seems impossible to surpass it. It is beautifully painted without and within; the construction is not only commodious and in the highest degree convenient, but displays good artistic taste and a liberal disbursement to secure the most beautiful woods and the most elegant furnishings. There are three state rooms and two drawing rooms in the car and one is at a loss which most to admire, the elegant black walnut cabinet work, the splendid mirrors, the warm, crimson velvet upholstery or the snug, convenient tables, lit as they are, so as to take from night travelling all its gloom and sombreness and instead of a tedious weary night's work between Toronto and Montreal to make it an agreeable evening in a very handsomely furnished first-class drawing room."

Annie Brassey, whose father-in-law, a notable British contractor, had built the Grand Trunk, travelled in one of these cars from Niagara to Toronto in 1871 and exclaimed over the fact that "lunch was served up, exactly like at a restaurant, all the cooking being done 'on the premises'."

Until this moment, all meals had had to be taken in station restaurants of varying quality. Sir Sandford Fleming, writing of the one in Truro, Nova Scotia, remarked that "one never criticizes railway meals too severely. . . . The golden rule on such occasions is to open your mouth, shut your eyes and take what is placed before you." Lady Monck, the governor's wife, whose husband was to become the first governor-general of the new nation, has left us a more enthusiastic description of several station meals in her journal of 1864. At Cobourg, Ontario, having slept on the train "very tolerably with our feet up on the bench opposite", she was treated to a breakfast of cold mutton chops "tasting of sheep and wool" and "delicious poached eggs and coffee." At Hamilton, she was so ravenous that "I ate first roast beef and then hot boiled mutton because there was no beef!" She added that "the dinners you get at railway stations in Canada are so much better than what you get when travelling at home." The food was "much more civilized . . . than . . . in civilized England where you rush in at stations to get old and cold soup and very horrid sandwiches."

In those days it was often the custom of travellers to provide and cook their own provisions. This was especially true of emigrants.

Sometimes uncooked provisions were provided on the Atlantic as part of the passage money, but most emigrants brought something of their own as well, since such voyages could last for eight weeks. On other ships, cooked food was served. Here is what emigrants aboard the steamer *Hibernia* ate during a typical day in 1872: At 8 a.m. coffee, bread and butter; at 12:30 potatoes and meat pudding (alternating on Fridays and Wednesdays with pea soup, salt fish, melted butter and potatoes); at 5 p.m. coffee, bread and butter; at 8 p.m. gruel. The bread was baked fresh, twice a day.

Even in the early days of the Canadian Pacific Railway travellers tended to bring along their own provisions. One observer tells of a group aboard a transcontinental train who brought "nothing less than all sorts of fare with tablecloths, tableware, wine and whiskey, a stove for making tea and the most amazing store of appetizing good things." Notwithstanding, all these people ate as well all the meals served in the dining car.

The excellence of the Canadian railway cuisine, which, with the advent of the Canadian Pacific Railway, was to achieve a world-wide reputation, probably goes back to the excellence of steamer fare on the lakes and rivers during the Confederation years. One of the great dishes of those days was broiled whitefish, served often enough on a plank with a matelote sauce.

"Palatial" was the word Lady Duffus Hardy used to describe the great steamboats that plied the St. Lawrence. In 1881 she travelled aboard one steamer out of Montreal which she said was like a four-storey house afloat "replete with the most luxurious accommodation with balconies running round every storey, elegant drawing rooms for the ladies, smoking and billiard rooms for the gentlemen and a capital cuisine for everybody's benefit." At mealtimes, as several wide-eyed travellers reported, the passengers fell on the food like a pack of wolves.

It was the CPR that made an event and an art out of dining on the move. In the eighties and nineties, following the driving of the last spike, all meals served on Canadian Pacific trains and boats could be had for a flat seventy-five cents. "It must be confessed," wrote one train traveller, "that you can get your money's worth at each of them if you give your mind to it regardless of consequence." There are ten courses listed on the SS *Alberta*'s dinner menu for August 11, 1887. The railway menus are a shade simpler, owing to the confined nature of the kitchens, but the luncheon menu for the same year between Winnipeg and Medicine Hat lists eight courses and a total of thirty-five dishes, all of which could be sampled for the one price.

As the decades rolled on Canadian railway dining became known the world over, for it was without doubt superior to any other. The mounds of crackling-crisp Canadian bacon, the evenly grilled Calgary sirloins, the plump, pink spring lamb chops, the succulent goldeyes with their melting pat of parsley butter, the juicy lakefish, slightly charred, the Oka and cheddar cheeses and the hot seasonal blueberry pies – all these came to be associated almost exclusively with our transcontinental train service. It is perhaps not too much to say that, if there is a distinctively Canadian style of cuisine, it is this; and not too surprising that, in an artificial nation bound together by bands of steel, it should spring directly from our dining cars.

"Corinthian" 1864

PLANKED WHITEFISH

Preheat a well-seasoned maple or oak plank 2 inches thick by pouring boiling water over it. Clean and split one **3-lb. whitefish**, remove backbone and lay fish flat on plank, skin side down. Season well with **salt, pepper** and **butter**. Broil 25 minutes, or bake in hot oven, basting occasionally with hot water mixed with butter and lemon juice. Serve with a **matelote sauce** (see below) or a butter sauce made with **½ cup butter, 1 tbsp. minced parsley,** and **1 tsp. lemon juice**. The fish should be sent to the table on the plank with mashed potatoes piped around the edge and mushrooms, tomatoes and other vegetables browned with the fish for a few minutes under the grill.

MATELOTE SAUCE
FOR
WHITEFISH

Sauté **1 onion** and **1 carrot**, both finely chopped, with **1 tbsp. butter**, until golden. Add **1 bay leaf, 1 clove garlic**, a dash of **thyme**, a handful of **mushroom peelings**, and the bones and head of the fish, chopped. Simmer for 10 minutes, then add **1 qt. red wine**. Cover pan. Cook until sauce is reduced to half. Strain through a fine sieve. Thicken with **1 tbsp. butter** and **1 tsp. flour**. Bring to a boil and add **1 tbsp. butter** before serving.

On Friday, August 19, 1864, George Tuthill Borrett, a fellow of King's College, Cambridge, wrote to his father in England this description of the St. Lawrence river boat that had just taken him from Quebec City to Montreal:

This was my first introduction to the river steamers of the New World, and truly they are an institution to which nothing that we have can for a moment be compared for comfort and speed combined. The American river-boat of which the Canadian is a copy is nothing more nor less than an immense floating hotel, a characteristic type of the people themselves, a curious combination of democratic follies and aristocratic propensities; a mixture of every kind of life – fast life, slow life, busy life, and lazy life, all under one roof. The saloon is a fine handsome room of great length and good height, fitted up with exaggerated decorations, extravagant and, as I think, tasteless. Along either side are the state cabins, each and all a good bedroom in itself, comfortably arranged and extremely well ventilated; and around them, on the outside, runs a sort of open deck or platform, where the passengers sit and promenade at their pleasure. At 6 p.m. dinner was served in the saloon, at the lower end, which is set apart as a dining-room, a handsome "high tea"; and after tea there was music, cards, chess and so on, till late in the evening, when, after a final moonlight walk outside, the passengers turned in.

In 1871, Mrs. Thomas Brassey, daughter-in-law of the Grand Trunk's builder and later a baroness, wrote with some disdain of the eating habits of "second and third-rate Americans" as she called them, aboard a St. Lawrence river steamer just out of Kingston:

Everybody stood round the room, leaning against the side of it, each with a chair behind them, which they had brought down from deck; no one being allowed to approach the table till the stewards in a loud voice announced, "Breakfast is now ready, ladies and gentlemen," upon which announcement they all flew at the table like a pack of hounds, and before we had time to approach, had cleaned (I can use no other word) the contents off every dish near them on to their own plates; and the gentlemen, in spite of the steward's remonstrances, paid no attention to any ladies – or females, as they call them here – but to those of their own party. Luckily the captain knew us, and after a little delay we had a separate breakfast served to us.

It was the custom in those days to sneer at the Yankees. In 1876, John J. Rowan, a somewhat snobbish Englishman writing for the benefit of those of his peers who might wish to emigrate, echoed the Baroness Brassey's words:

Even the American tourists who travel in Canada for amusement and economy – for strange as it may seem, it is cheaper to travel in Canada than to live at home in the United States – are not of a stamp likely to charm Canadians into annexation. The better classes of Americans do not travel on the beautiful Canadian lakes, for fear of the rough and motley crowd of their own countrymen that they encounter on the steamboats. I do not think these latter people derive much enjoyment from the scenery of "Kennedy", as they call it, although they undoubtedly enjoy the good living. I recently had the pleasure of travelling in company with some four hundred of these tourists. One hour before dinner, though at the time our boat was running down one of the finest reaches of the St. Lawrence, these people crowded the dinner tables in the saloon. The waiters told them that unless they left the tables, the cloth, &c., could not be laid. Upon this they drew back their chairs a foot or two to enable the waiters to pass to and fro, and there they sat for one hour, their hungry regards fixed on the table, their blackpanted extremities tucked under their chairs, like rows of carrion crows waiting for a dying horse. At last dinner was put on the table, and a fierce joy lit up the solemn, yellow faces of the four hundred, and in the words of the captain they "went it strong", so strong indeed that the outsiders preferred bread and cheese on deck to partaking of that horrid repast.

In 1881 Lady Duffus Hardy, another titled Englishwoman, travelling on another St. Lawrence river steamer, described her first encounter with one native Canadian dish:

I lean back on my luxurious lounge in a rather sleepy state, and am fast drifting away into a land of dreams, when I am roused by the loud prolonged sound of the dinner-gong, and we all crowd down, helter-skelter, to the dining saloon, where our captain, a big burly man, sits at the head of the table, with sundry roasts and fancy dishes smoking before him. We speedily spoil our appetites, and leave but a mere wreck of bare bones and skeletons. One dish contains Indian corn cobs about a quarter of a yard long, looking white and tempting with their granulated covering. Believing they are some stuffed delicacies, I ask for a small piece. A smile goes round, and I receive a whole one on my plate. What am I to do with it? I glance at my neighbours. Every one is holding a cob with his two hands, and, beginning at one end, nibbles along as though he were playing a flute till he gets to the other, repeating the process till the cob is stripped of its pearly corn. I don't think it is worth the trouble of eating, though it is considered a great dainty on this side of the Atlantic.

Sir Sandford Fleming, the greatest of all Canadian railway surveyors, has supplied us with this description of his attempts to get breakfast on a lake steamer between Collingwood and Owen Sound:

The breakfast hour is seven, but I had had some experience of the preceding evening's supper. Appetite must possess to many a somewhat tyrannical mastery, if we are to judge by the demonstrative determination to obtain seats at a steamboat table. With us there were four relays of supper, and it was an effort to find a seat at any one of them. Who has not noticed, under such circumstances, the rows of men and women who place themselves, with suppressed impatience, behind the seats, standing in the most prosaic of attitudes, in expectation for the word that the meal is ready. I was myself content to take my place at the fourth table, so that I could eat what I required with deliberation. With this experience, I was in no hurry to rise, so it was about nine o'clock when I entered the long saloon. There were a

HOW TO MAKE
MOCK OYSTERS
OUT OF
CANADIAN CORN

Grate ½ **doz. ears of corn** with a coarse grater, beat the whites and yolks of **3 eggs** and add them to the corn, with **1 tbsp. flour**, **1 tbsp. butter**, **1 tsp. salt**, and **pepper** to taste. Stir well and drop spoonsful of this batter into a frying pan with hot butter and lard (or vegetable shortening) and fry a light brown on both sides.

~ Canada's Favorite Cook Book, 1907

The Duchess,
Columbia River stern-wheeler,
B.C., circa 1887

MONTREAL PUDDING

Beat and strain **3 eggs** through a sieve and mix them with ½ **cup milk**, **2 oz. brown sugar** and ½ **tsp. nutmeg**. Gradually add ¼ **lb. flour**, mixing well. Then stir in **7 oz. bread crumbs** and beat all together for at least half an hour before putting it into the saucepan. Well butter an earthen mould, or basin, put in the mixture, tie it tightly over and let it boil 3 hours without stopping. For a change, ½ **lb. stoned raisins** may be added.

~ Warwick's Everyday Cookery, Toronto, circa 1870

Authors' note: We think that Montreal can now do better than this.

TORONTO PIE

Mix **1 cup sugar**, **3 eggs**, **1½ cups flour** and **1 tsp. baking powder**. Bake as for a jelly cake in layers and spread between the layers raspberry jam.

~ The Home Cook Book, Toronto, 1877

Authors' note: This makes a pretty stiff batter. In our opinion it would be improved by cutting amount of flour in half. Bake 15 minutes at 375°.

few stragglers like myself present, probably influenced by the same philosophy, who were seated here and there at a table on which lay the scattered remains of the fourth breakfast. On these lake boats the attendants are called "waiters", not "stewards" as on ocean steamers, and if there be a difference of nomenclature, there is certainly no identity of manner. The steward of the ocean steamer is the most benignant, courtly, kindly, considerate person in the world, and, as a rule, his virtues in this respect are sufficiently appreciated. On this boat I addressed one of the waiters, I thought politely enough, and gave my orders. I was met by the rugged reply, in the hardest of tones, "Ye cannot have hot breakfasts if ye lie in bed." The man's axiom was certainly borne out by fact. There was no breakfast, in the sense of the word, and what there remained was not hot. But the coffee was exceptionally good, and with a crust of bread I thought that I might have fared worse. Possibly the owners of the new steamers to be placed on the lakes next summer will introduce some improvement in the stewards' department, which the ordinary traveller, they may be assured, will duly appreciate.

In the 70s, the Governor-General's wife, Lady Dufferin, described her own preparations for a train trip to Western Canada:

The week has been spent in arranging for our departure for the Grand Tour. A great difference of opinion exists as to what we shall want en route. Some say take provisions, others say don't. We decided, however, in the first place, to have a box made to hold plates, cups and saucers, knives and forks, tea, salt, etc. Then we take cases of preserved meats, a basket of eggs, some butter, Devonshire cream, and jam, and we have a refrigerator in our baggage-car. So we shan't starve, as we can add our own delicacies to the tough antelope-steaks we are to get on the way.

Sir Sandford Fleming has left us several acerb descriptions of refreshment station meals in the early days of the Canadian Pacific Railway, before the dining car became a standard fixture. Here is one of them:

The passengers begin to be clamorous for the next refreshment station. We learn that it is at Rat Portage. We trust that the name does not suggest the cheer we are to receive. There is an old tradition that the Chinaman delighted in that rodent, and we all have read that during the siege of Paris it was an established article of food. . . . When the train came to a stand the proverbial rush for dinner was made. No regular refreshment room could be found. In fact, none had yet been erected. But there were several temporary shanties built around, whose merits were loudly proclaimed by the several touts in a great many words and the ringing of bells. . . . We selected one of these establishments. Our recollections of Rat Portage are not impressed by any excellence in its commissariat. That which was set before us was execrable. I am not difficult to please, but there is a lower depth in these matters. Such a meal would scarcely have been palatable during the hunger of the siege of Paris, and a man could only have swallowed what was given at Rat Portage when suffering the pangs of starvation. There is evidently a call for improvement at this place before the line is fully opened to travellers.

Shortly after the CPR was completed, the English traveller Edward Roper, journeying from Montreal to Winnipeg for a fare of just eight dollars, left this description of his first visit to the dining car:

The "diner" itself is just as handsome in its way as the "sleeper". On either side a passage, nicely carpeted, is a row of tables; some seat two, some four. At one end is a kitchen, which must be very perfect in its arrangements, for they appear to be able to do any kind of cooking in it, from baking fancy bread and cakes and roasting meat to all the niceties that one could find "ashore".

They talk of a train in America, and in Canada too, as they would of a ship. It is "All aboard" where in England it would be "Take your seats!" and, consequently, "Get on board," "Come on board," &c. They say "ship some freight"; for the goods, you see, become "freight" here. It is a "freight train" which is loaded with goods. One speaks of "ahead" and "astern" of the train; so why not "ashore", to keep up the metaphor?

The table furniture of the dining-car is quite complete, the service excellent, and decidedly better than in most hotels in that country. The waiters are polite, there is no hurry, the cooking is excellent, and the charge is uniformly 72 cents (3 s.); considering everything, a most reasonable charge.

The bill of fare does not vary greatly, except with the season and locality. For example, here in Ontario, the white fish (very delicious) and lake trout take the place of salmon farther west on the Pacific slope. The fruits here are only oranges and apples now, but as we draw near the end of our journey we shall probably find bananas, apricots and peaches.

We had already adopted the general Canadian custom of beginning breakfast with fruit. Most people take also porridge and milk, usually spoken of there as "oatmeal", but we English did not seem to relish it. After that came *lamb* chops (which it is not Canadian etiquette to call *mutton*), fried *chicken* (you must not say *fowl*), beef-steak, veal cutlets, ham, which last is far from good in Canada, and what they call English breakfast bacon, which is seldom so good as what we are accustomed to in England. Eggs, of course, in every style, various kinds of bread, rolls, Johnny cakes, buck-wheat cakes, and buns, with coffee, chocolate, and "English breakfast tea". It is evident, therefore, that we had a very fair choice of viands, and I believe that we were well pleased with our first "Square" meal on wheels. . . .

BREAD SAUCE
(FOR POULTRY OR GAME)

Take all the **giblets** from a fowl, place in **1 pint of water** and add **1 onion, 10 whole peppers** and **1 blade of mace.** (Use ½ tsp. powdered mace.) Simmer for 1 hour, then strain the liquor over ¾ **lb. bread crumbs.** Place in a stewpan, cover and let it stand over a low heat without boiling for 1 hour. Beat with a fork until smooth. Boil for 5 minutes, stirring well until thick, add **2 tbsps. cream** and serve hot.

~ Mrs. Clarke's Cookery Book, Toronto, 1883

PINEAPPLE FRITTERS

Make a thick and smooth batter with ¾ **pint cream,** the yolks and whites of **3 eggs,** separately beaten, a pinch of **salt** and sufficient **flour** to make it a proper consistency. Peel **1 pineapple,** slice it and let slices soak in **1 cup curaçoa,** mixed with **2½ oz. powdered sugar,** for several hours. When well flavoured with the liqueur, dip the pieces into the thick batter and fry on each side in boiling fat. When done, drain them on white blotting-paper before the fire to absorb the grease. Serve on a white doilie and sift loaf sugar over them quickly.

~ Warwick's Everyday Cookery, Toronto, circa 1870

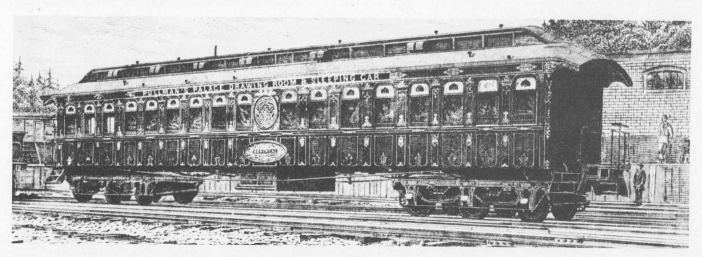

Pullman's first Palace Car, October 1870

QUINTE CHEDDAR

ERMITE

CAMEMBERT   FRUILANO   OKA

BABY GOUDA   VERY OLD CHEDDAR

❁ ❁ ❁
NEW WINE
&
OLD CHEESE
❁

Canadian cheeses are the finest in the world, as anyone who has nibbled on a piece of sharp cheddar or Oka knows. Canadian wines are something else again. Yet for anybody who wants a cold summer punch or a hot winter drink, they are an excellent buy. For large, gay parties, try these money savers.

THE DRINKS

HOT SPICED WINE: (*left foreground*) Dissolve 1 cup sugar in 3 cups boiling water. Add rind of half a lemon, 18 cloves and a 6-inch stick of cinnamon. Boil 15 minutes. Strain into double boiler, add 2 large bottles Canadian claret. Serve piping hot with nutmeg. For ten persons.

SUMMER PUNCH: (*right foreground in jug*) Mix 1 bottle sparkling rosé, 1 bottle Seven-Up, 1 bottle soda and ½ cup brandy. Garnish with cherries. Serves six.

SANGAREE: (*background in giant snifter*) Fill a tumbler with chipped ice, add 1 tsp. powdered sugar and juice of half a lemon. Fill tumbler with claret, shake, add an orange slice, sprinkle nutmeg on top and drink it through a straw.

SHERRIED BOUILLON ON THE ROCKS: (*in footed goblet, centre*) Place 2 ice-cubes in a glass, add undiluted condensed bouillon from a tin, stir in 1 tbsp. sherry and garnish with a lemon slice.

THE CHEESES

CAMEMBERT (*Canadian version*): A dessert cheese, it's best at room temperature. Serve with a dry wine.

FRUILANO: A Canadian version of an Italian cheese. For luncheon or snacks. It's very mild.

OKA: The pride of Quebec, this is a Port Salud, made by Trappist monks. Soft and highly flavoured.

ERMITE: A blue cheese made by Benedictine monks at St. Benoit, Quebec. Excellent after a meal, with red wine.

BABY GOUDA: Canadians now make this Dutch cheese, which, being very, very mild, is best for luncheons or snacks.

CHEDDAR: The best varieties come from Eastern Ontario: The geology of the land produces the best grass, hence the best milk, hence the best cheese.

Wines, Courtesy Jordan Wines Ltd.; Cheeses, The Old World Cheese Shop, Toronto

4/The Temperance Era

Illustration for "A Temperance Lecture",
Toronto Saturday Night, *New Year's Eve, 1887*

"How welcome it is," wrote Annie Macpherson, an English charity worker, in 1870, "to see at every Canadian's table the wholesome cup of tea at dinner as well as supper and not the ever-ensnaring glass of wine as at home!"

Perhaps. Yet, if our ancestors had drunk more good wine with their meals and less raw whisky before and after, our culinary heritage would certainly have been richer. To this day wine is an exception on Canadian tables and in Canadian cooking and we have our pioneer background to blame for it.

At the time of Confederation, beer and wine were all but unknown, though, ironically, one Canadian vintage from Cooksville, Ontario, won a gold medal at the Paris Exposition of 1867. This must have been a fluke: the Baroness Brassey, dining at Montreal's St. Lawrence Hall, reported that "the wine was infamous, which is always the case here: most of the inhabitants seem to drink iced water with their meals and then go into the bar 'to have a drink'." They do so to this very day.

Bad, cheap whisky was the curse of our pioneer days. It caused so much misery, so much poverty, so much rowdyism and drunkenness that it swiftly gave rise to the fierce backlash of the temperance movement, which was eventually to render Canadian cuisine spiritless. Even as late as the 1950s a Toronto immigrant restaurateur, who knew no better, was fined $200 for slipping a drop or two of kirsch into his fruit salad.

Today we tend to sneer at the temperance societies with their naive carols about "the strength cold water brings", but we forget the conditions that brought them into being. Heavy drinking was an accepted pioneer custom and every bee, wedding, election, funeral and political rally was washed down with gallons of whisky. A few years before Confederation you could buy a glass of raw rye for a penny. When Canada was formed it cost about a nickel – for as much as you could gulp without taking breath. Often enough it was free: many a store had an open barrel at the back with a dipper hanging beside it. Canadians were perhaps the hardest drinkers in the world. In

1840 a visiting temperance lecturer declared that Toronto was worse than any other town of its size on the continent. It did not improve. By 1876 one visitor remarked on "the startling frequency of drinking shops. . . . Every other little store is licensed to sell Ale, Wine and Spirituous Liquors. Very often there are two together; sometimes there are actually four." On the road from Toronto to Barrie, Edwin Guillet tells us, there was a tavern every mile of the way. A farmer, bringing pigs to market, could treat the entire crowd for a quarter and since treating was encouraged by the saloonkeepers a man might be obliged to down a dozen drinks before he staggered out to the wagon where his shivering wife awaited him.

Saloonkeepers had a habit of standing on the sidewalks urging passersby to enter and "almost forcibly propelling them," in the memory of J. V. McAree, the Toronto columnist. Since drink was cheap it was in the saloonkeepers' interests to urge the customers to consume more than was good for them. The spectacle of drunkenness on the streets was a common one, accounting for the majority of arrests. "There was hardly an arrest that was not a disgusting and shocking spectacle," McAree remembered. "Today people would consider it horrifying. . . . The prisoner would usually be pretty helpless and would have to be half-dragged, half-carried by the police. It was the same with women. Perhaps most of the prisoners would do their best to stagger along beside the policeman, followed by a crowd of youngsters. With others it was a point of honour to put up the strongest resistance."

Tales of rowdyism on holidays and at fair time are numberless. The *Brant Review* of October 10, 1885, describing the scenes following the fall fair at Paris, Ontario, reported the main street "was almost blocked by a drunken, cursing, howling mob." This was typical, for whisky was the universal panacea, stimulant, painkiller, boredom reliever and psychological reinforcement of those days. It was everything, in short, save an appetizer.

Many a farmer and workman drank himself into bankruptcy and it is not surprising that, by Confederation, the strong and enthusiastic temperance movement was already well established. The "old pledge" societies, whose members believed in real temperance and allowed for an occasional glass of wine and beer, had been replaced by the inflexible "new pledge" groups, which believed in total abstinence. By the 1860s women were being admitted and their presence helped turn "the damned cold water drinking societies" into social organizations. Temperance hotels sprang up for those travellers who could not stomach the presence of a bar. Suddenly it became more respectable to be a temperance man than a tippler.

"The reader will notice that I make no mention of anything like strong drink," wrote Edward Roper, describing a camping trip up the north arm of Burrard Inlet, near Vancouver, in 1887. "It is the very last thing anyone thinks about on such an expedition – anyone who considers himself respectable, I mean. I don't suppose any of us were teetotallers, but temperance is clearly the rule in that country; and I believe none of us thought of anything stronger than tea, which we drank in large quantities, hot and cold but always potent."

Two other travellers, J. A. Lees and W. J. Clutterbuck, a year later described an experience in the Queen's Hotel, a small log building in New Westminster: "We found on the table in the sitting room a sedately bound volume of considerable bulk, entitled *Reveries of a Bachelor,* new edition. This implied a neatly veiled compliment to married men, for the book was nothing but an ingenious dodge for evading the N.W. drink regulations. A secret spring was revealed to us by the landlord disclosing the neck of a whisky bottle most artfully concealed within the leaves."

Such subterfuge became increasingly necessary as the temperance movement gained power and the laws were changed to accommodate it. As Douglas Sladen reported in 1895, even the *idea* of serving so much as a glass of wine with food was considered *de trop.* At every social gathering, he wrote, "the blight of the Prohibition Act hung over all the festivities which generally consisted of tea and fruit and confectionary and ice cream and introductions." No host "was unregenerate enough to offer us a 'square drink' even though the weather made it as easy to raise a thirst as if one had been east of Suez." And so, for the next generation, most of the country was as dry as the Sahara and much of the food as pallid as straw.

Tracts by the bushel
Beer by the barrel

*Paradoxically, beer and temperance tracts
were both more plentiful in Victorian Canada
than they are today.*

*When George Brown of Halifax raced Evan Morris of Pittsburgh on the
Kennebecasis river near Saint John, N.B., on September 26, 1874,
the spectators arriving by the early train could buy beer from the barrel
in unlimited quantities. Books about "The Old Vice and the New Chivalry"
were designed to prevent such excesses. The fact that beer cannot be
sold today at any outdoor sports event in Canada suggests that they succeeded.*

PIONEER
BLACKBERRY WINE

Crush the berries with a wooden pestle in a wooden tub or bucket; draw off all the juice and add to it an equal quantity of water and two pounds of refined sugar for each gallon in the mixture. Keep it in jars till the fermentation is complete and then bottle and cork it up. A second fermentation will take place in the ensuing spring, during which another pound of sugar should be added to each gallon. The wine thus prepared will keep well and improve by age.

~ The Canadian Illustrated News, Sept. 2, 1871

DANDELION WINE

To **1 qt. dandelion flowers**, take **2 qts. boiling water** and pour over the flowers. Let stand over night, strain next day and add **3 lbs. sugar** to **1 gallon juice** and **2 lemons**. Bring the whole to a boil, then put into a barrel or keg and add **yeast** to work. Keep enough juice to fill up as required. When through working it must be tightly corked.

~ The New Galt Cookbook, 1898

RHUBARB WINE

To each **gallon of soft water** take **5 lbs. rhubarb** cut fine but not peeled. Let this stand 10 days, then strain through a muslin cloth and add **4 lbs. white sugar** to each gallon of juice plus the rind and juice of **1 lemon**. As soon as the sugar is dissolved, bottle. Put corks in loose.

~ The New Galt Cookbook, 1898

On July 15, 1867, The Canadian Farmer proudly quoted the Moniteur Vinicole of France, an established authority, on the subject of the wine specimens sent to the Paris Exhibition by the St. Clair Association of Cooksville, Ontario:

"Canada, of which we have not yet spoken, so small is its importance as a wine-growing country, has nevertheless drawn our attention by the display of the produce of the vine-harvest of Upper Canada. It is because this exhibition is unique that we felt ourselves obliged to recognize it; and well it was that we did so, for of all the wines that we have tasted not made in France, it certainly is that which approaches nearest to the nature of our *vin ordinaire*. It is at the foot of a hill that has been planted a vineyard of about fifteen hectares, and the plantation has been in existence for seven years. . . . The wine is that which we call in France a *vin gris*, the pale red of which, by its body and its colour even, and by its strength, shows that it is only a year old. By its taste, its *bouquet* and its . . . *franchise*, it approaches the light wines of Beaujolais . . ."

On July 3, 1867, the Toronto Leader reported on the aftermath of Dominion Day festivities in neighbouring Hamilton:

The city has shaken down again into its staid old habits. There was a remarkable absence of drunkenness on Dominion Day, and the behaviour of the people generally was worthy of all praise. It appeared to be reserved for the race course to show the worst example, and strangely enough, although no liquor tents were on the ground, there was more than the usual amount of drunkenness. The great cry was for places of refreshment, and the dust being heavy it was disagreeable – nothing, not even water to quench the thirst; yet there were many drunken persons abroad, and no less than six fights occurred the first day . . ."

Thomas Conant of Oshawa, whose grandfather fought in the rebellion of 1837 and who collected pioneer settler stories, wrote, later in his life, of the One-Thousand-and-One Society, which sprang up at the time of Confederation:

The "One-Thousand-and-One Society" of those days was an organization formed among those who habitually drank and spent nights at bouts, and was a recognized order among them. Probably there never was any written constitution or by-laws to govern them; still the rules of the society were as well known and as fully recognized as if there were such. The fundamental rule which they were to observe in their drinking was that no one must drink more than two gallons at one sitting without rising and reporting the matter to the recognized chiefs of the order.

We must, in all charity, believe that the liquid in this case would be beer – in any case it could hardly be spirits; still I am led to believe, in many instances, before the great goal of the two gallons was reached, the beer would be frequently mixed with spirits.

In British Columbia, Milton and Cheadle reported how one Cariboo miner dispensed his fortune among a crowd in a Victoria saloon:

One man who, at the end of the season, found himself possessed of 30,000 or 40,000 dollars, having filled his pockets with twenty-dollar gold pieces, on his arrival in Victoria proceeded to a "bar-room," and treated "the crowd" to champagne. The company present being unable to consume all the bar-keeper's stock, assistance was obtained from without, and the passers-by compelled to come in. Still the supply held out, and not another "drink" could any one swallow. In this emergency the ingenious giver of the treat ordered every glass belonging to the establishment to be brought out and filled. Then raising his stick, with one fell swoop he knocked the army of glasses off the counter. One hamper of champagne, however, yet remained, and, determined not to be beaten, he ordered it to be opened and placed upon the floor, and jumping in, stamped the bottles to pieces beneath his heavy boots, severely cutting his shins, it is said, in the operation. But although the champagne was at last finished, he had a handful of gold pieces to dispose of, and walking up to a large mirror, worth several hundred dollars, which adorned one end of the room, dashed a shower of heavy coins against it, and shivered it to pieces. The hero of this story returned to the mines the following spring without a cent, and was working as a common labourer at the time of our visit. A freak of one of the most successful Californians may be appended as a companion to the story just related. When in the height of his glory he was in the habit of substituting champagne bottles – full ones, too – for the wooden pins in the bowling alley, smashing batch after batch with infinite satisfaction to himself, amid the applause of his companions and the "bar-keep."

John J. Rowan, the English sportsman, had no use for the temperance movement, which dogged him during his travels through Canada, circa 1876. In spite of his strange encounter with a drunken hotelkeeper, he felt the temperance idea was an impractical one:

The little hotels in the backwoods, as might be expected, are rather rough. I had the misfortune to be travelling at night once in the lower province in a tremendous snow storm; our horses done out, pitch dark, and very cold. We were blundering through the drifts at the rate of a mile an hour. "How far to the nearest stopping place?" I asked the driver. "Only a mile," he replied. This cheered me up somewhat, and I said, "Oh, that's all right, we'll soon be there;" but my cheerfulness was not shared by my driver. On my asking what sort of hotel it was, he made the following mysterious reply: "First-rate, when Dickey's not on the beer." In my innocence I imagined that any hotel or house, even if Dickey was "on the beer," would be all right. I soon found my mistake. On arrival at the "hotel," I opened the door of a comfortable-looking house, and was on the point of ordering supper, when an immense fellow, brandishing the leg of a chair, and backed up by half-a-dozen drunken companions, made at me, and with terrific threats ordered me out. A man who is half frozen as well as tired and hungry is not much in the humour to fight, so "I retired." My driver had already made off. He told me afterwards that Dickey had once killed a hungry traveller, but that when not "on the beer" he was one of the whitest men on the earth.

A thirsty man, with an empty pocket, opposite a fountain : Result—A hearty drink, a clear head, a healthy stomach, pocket as before.

A tippler, with a shilling and no thirst, opposite a bottle of whiskey : Result—Stupefaction, fever, dyspepsia, and an empty pocket.

Sketched in a B.C. mining camp, circa 1887

There is a strong party in Ontario who believe that it would be an advantage to apply the Maine Liquor Law to their province. These people cannot find much to encourage them across the border in those states where it has been tried. I believe that one reason why Canadians are a healthier and more robust race than the Yankees is that they drink better liquor. Perhaps they would be better still if they drank none at all; I do not venture to offer an opinion on this point, but we know that men will have alcoholic stimulant, and prohibitory laws have never banished the bars from Maine or Massachusetts, though they have driven them to the cellar and the attic. They have never prevented drinking, though they have made men drink in a skulking, guilty way, as if they were about to commit a murder or a robbery. They have had the effect, however, of damaging the liquor and making it poisonous. It is misfortune for paupers to marry and beget pauper children; granted; but try and check the pauper population by prohibitory laws, and the result will be a still worse quality of pauperism. If the good people who shout so lustily under the temperance banner would only turn their energies towards substituting good unadulterated liquor in place of alcoholic poison they would do good service. At present they are spending their time, their brains, and their money in an attempt which is about as impracticable as to check the ebb and flow of the tide.

Another British traveller and writer, Peter O'Leary, who visited Canada within a year of Rowan, took a more pious approach. O'Leary reported to prospective emigrants that "sobriety is the one thing essential to success and unless a man keeps from whisky he is almost sure to go to the dogs." His experience in Montreal confirmed him in his beliefs:

There are a great many hotels and saloons in Montreal. To the latter the citizens are very much opposed, and although hotels are useful, and as American and Canadian society is constituted they are even necessary, still their drink-selling licence ought to be restricted, as well as that of their less important neighbours. I am very glad to say that drinking is not looked upon as the correct thing, and that drunkards, high and low, are generally treated with contempt, and serve them right, for, if a man is so corrupt or diseased that for the sake of gratifying his appetite he will sink below the level of the beast, such a man cannot be a good citizen or a good Christian. As a rule the natives are very temperate, but a large portion of the Europeans keep up their old drinking habits. I went through the city prison, accompanied by the Deputy Governor. There were 325 prisoners, and full half of them suffering on account of offences committed when under the influence of drink. . . . My companion told me that intoxicating liquors were the source of filling the prison with poor unfortunate creatures, who in most cases would be good members of society, only for the baneful influence of the public-house, and he gave me his permission to make this fact known wherever I could. There are several temperance organizations, and a society formed to curtail the liquor traffic.

During his travels in the Northwest Territories in 1880, the correspondent of The Times, W. Fraser Rae, had occasion to remark on the act of prohibition that prevailed "out of consideration for the Indians and in continuance of the policy of the Hudson's Bay Company":

Owing to attempts to defeat the operation of such an Act the definition of intoxicants is made to include every conceivable form of intoxicating beverage or solid substance, the words of the Act being: "The expression 'intoxicating liquor' shall mean and include all spirits, strong waters, spiritous liquors, wines, fermented or compounded liquors or intoxicating fluids; and the expression 'intoxicant' shall include opium or any preparation thereof, and any other intoxicating drug or substance, and tobacco or tea mixed, compounded or impregnated with opium, or with any other intoxicating drug, spirit or substance, and whether the same or any of them be liquid or solid." Though not himself a total abstainer on principle, the Governor has become one during his term of office on the ground that he could not well enforce the Act if he made himself an exception to its provisions. He is beset with applications for licences; indeed, the enforcement of the law against the use of intoxicants gives him more annoyance and labour than any other of his duties. He thinks the prohibitive system works well on the whole. Whether it can be upheld when the country is more densely populated remains to be seen. The newly-arrived settlers complain bitterly about the Act. An English farmer's wife told me that she missed her glass of beer at dinner more than anything else, and that if she could enjoy it again, she would not regret having left her old home.

But the act was often honoured in the breach, as Stuart Cumberland, the geographer, discovered when he crossed the plains in 1887 by rail:

Despite the efforts of the scarlet-coated police, who have an observing eye and a keenly discriminating nose, there is a good deal of illicit traffic in spirits going on in the Territory; and I don't wonder at the most law-respecting person running the risk of fine, imprisonment, or even decapitation in seeking to give a tone to his stomach by means of stimulants after going through a course of the vile non-intoxicants which are allowed by law to be sold to unsuspecting travellers.

These decoctions go by the names of 'spruce beer', 'botanic ale', and 'Moose-Jaw beer'; and, whilst each of these bottled horrors is warranted not to intoxicate, the unhappy purchaser receives no warranty as to what other consequences may arise from the drinking of them.

Some people thrive on these 'drinks', I suppose, otherwise there would be no sale for them; whilst I have seen travellers grow quite husky and weak about the knees after drinking from a bottle labelled 'botanic ale', and grow cheerful and familiar with sipping at a bottle resplendent in a label describing its contents as non-intoxicating 'Moose-Jaw beer'.

In a thirsty moment I ventured upon obtaining a bottle of one of these harmless decoctions. I drank some of it, but, strange to say, I felt neither merry nor husky; and thinking I had not taken enough of it, I swallowed the remainder at a go. Then the trouble began. My mind

HOW THE AUTHORS MAKE HARD CIDER

Buy a ten-gallon white oak cask with a bung hole in the side and a small cork-sized hole bored in the top. From a chemical supply shop get a rubber cork to fit the hole, with an eight-inch glass tube running through it. To this tube attach several feet of rubber tubing. Put **8½ gals. sweet cider** in the barrel through the bung hole. Add **1 lb. sticky raisins.** Warm one extra gallon of cider on the stove and slowly dissolve in it **10 lbs. white sugar.** Add this to the barrel. Fill any remaining space with sweet cider and ram the bung in place. Run the rubber tube from the cork into a milk bottle full of water. The cider will start working at once and will bubble into the water. This prevents air from reaching the cider and souring it.

The cider will work for approximately two weeks and should then be ready to bottle. Each bottle should contain a little **acetylsalicylic acid** (aspirin) to "fix" it. Cork bottles well and lay on side in a cool place. The longer the cider keeps, the better.

JUGGED RABBIT
WITH SHERRY

Take two skinned, drawn rabbits, wash carefully and carve as you would a chicken. Roll in **4 tbsps. flour. Melt ½ cup butter** in a frying pan and add the meat. Brown well on both sides being careful not to burn. When meat is well browned, place it in a stewpan. Add the rest of the flour to the butter in the frying pan and stir until the mixture is smooth. Add 3 cups of water and cook for 10 minutes. Pour this liquid over the meat in the stewpan, add **1 onion,** uncut, **2 bay leaves, 3 whole cloves, 1 tsp. allspice, 1 tbsp. salt, ½ tsp. pepper.** Close cover and simmer for an hour and a half. Then add **4 tbsp. sherry, 1 tbsp. lemon juice** and **1 tbsp. condensed mushroom soup.** Arrange rabbit on a hot platter and strain the sauce over it. Serve with boiled rice.
For 6 persons.

~ The Royal Victoria Cook Book, Barrie, Ont., 1900

went immediately back to the shellfish on the banks of the Fraser, whilst in body I writhed about on the sofa in the saloon carriage. Opposite to me sat a sturdy rancher with a particularly fine glowing nose, and although he had a few moments before been drinking out of a 'botanic ale' bottle, he seemed the picture of jollity and ease. How I envied that man his evident peace of mind – and body! and I began to calculate how many years it would take before one got seasoned to the stuff so as to look and feel as he did.

By-and-by, noticing my distress, he spoke to me.

'Look here,' he said, 'just you take a nip of this; it will soon put you all right.'

But the very sight of the label turned me sick, and I shook my head sadly but determinedly.

'No? Oh, I suppose it's t'other sort you want?' and by way of increasing my horror he held out a 'spruce beer' bottle. This was too much for me, and with a shudder I closed my eyes.

Presently I felt the cold rim of a bottle touch my lips, and a smell stronger than that of either 'spruce beer', 'botanic ale,' or even 'Moose-Jaw beer' filled my nostrils. With this revival was immediate; but on looking up, the man, instead of offering me his brandy flask, was still holding out the bottle labelled 'Spruce beer – non-intoxicant'.

It did not take long to take in the situation, and soon we were having a friendly chat, in which he told me that his 'botanic ale' bottle contained good Scotch whisky – 'real Highland, and none of that Bourbon rubbish'. He also gave me the signs by which I might secure similar strong drinks when visiting wayside refreshment-rooms in the Territory. But which eye you have to wink for Scotch and which for Irish, and how many fingers you hold up for brandy, I am not going to tell. Travellers in the Territory will soon find all this out, as not even a Verdant Green could be there long without being initiated.

Edward Roper, whose reports on his travels in Canada have enlivened several chapters in this book, was dead set against the temperance movement and attacked it amusingly in his book By Track and Trail. At Lorne Park, then a summer resort near Toronto, he discovered that all liquor was banned. In Winnipeg he had to engage in subterfuge to get a drink on Sunday. Yet, as the final item below shows, he did not feel that Canadians were the boozers that his countrymen were:

"One of the cardinal principles of the company is that *no intoxicating liquors* are allowed, under any circumstances, to be sold at the hotel or refreshment booths, or on board the steamer running to the park." So says the official circular or guide issued by the management, and I was told that the directors purpose forbidding the sale and use of tobacco too! It is a "moral" park, run on hyper-moralistic principles. There no sin is to enter, all is to be peace; the drum and fife of the wicked world is not to be heard.

There is, I suppose, some church organization at the bottom of it, and no doubt *there* will be set a most beautiful example to the rest of the Canadian world; for at home, amongst the "brethren," how saint-like is the life of the members; abroad, amongst their fellowmen, they are very much like other human beings. The social cigar, the lively lager, the nimble dollar, have exactly the same value in their eyes as in those of their non-professing brothers.

The next day, Sunday, I had a terrible cold, and went about in misery. Towards night I remarked to a man "if I was in a civilized land I could get some whisky hot, which would do one good; but here, where your liquor law forbids its sale on Sunday I must suffer." "Come with me and see," he said.

So we went down a back street and up a narrow alley into a place where there was a bar room in full swing, crowded with people drinking.

At the bar I said, "I'll take whisky hot." The gay bar tender put on a serious look, "Sir, don't you know it is Sunday? We can't sell drinks, except to people who take their food here. This is a restaurant!"

My companion winked to me, and we went to the dining room and munched a biscuit, then ordering and being served with what intoxicants we pleased.

It is thus they circumvent the law in Winnipeg.

In Canada there is, perhaps, as much drunkenness as in England; but there certainly is not that constant "boozing"; men do not stupify themselves with beer here. A British workman seems to think it is his bounden duty to consume all the beer he can get.

In Canada this is not the case. Large districts are entirely without places where beer is sold, and even where it is not so, where people can get what they choose to drink, they do not soak themselves in beer. If anyone did, he would be looked on as a very black sheep indeed, even by his mates; would not be trusted, and would not be employed.

So it is that when our people get there, if they are not lost to all that is good, they fall into Canadian ways, and become very quickly far more respectable members of society than they were before; either that, or they go headlong to the dogs. There seems to be small chance of any middle course out there.

In Victoria, plenty of drink could be got with ease, just as in England, yet amongst the working-people, old-country people principally, there was usually a smartness, clearness of perception, which I attribute greatly to that pernicious custom of beer-drinking being out of fashion there. No woman, not the very lowest, ever enters a barroom or drinking saloon in any part of Canada. They set themselves up very greatly, men and women, on the proprieties.

J. V. McAree, in his Globe and Mail column of May 2, 1953, recalled the world of the saloon as it was when he was a boy in Toronto in the 1880s:

What I saw, with few exceptions that served to set out the general pattern, were proprietors and bartenders whose philosophy was "If I don't sell him whisky someone else will." However poor, young or old, sober or drunk, whatever he would buy they would sell. When he got drunk they short-changed him; when he was broke or too drunk to spend more they put him out to stagger home, sometimes first rolled by the bartender or the hangers-on. The big money came from the working man who got home drunk late Saturday night after having left most of his pay in the saloons downtown.

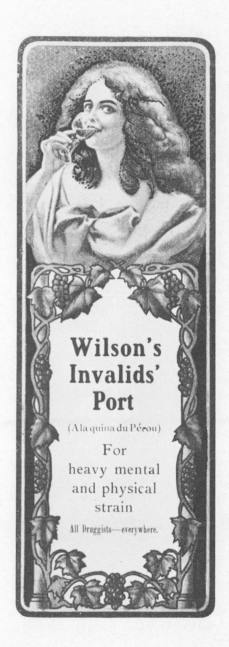

Wilson's Invalids' Port

(A la quina du Pérou)

For heavy mental and physical strain

All Druggists—everywhere.

TIPSY CAKE

Scoop the centre carefully out of a **moulded sponge cake** so as to leave the shape intact and fill with **strawberry preserve**. Cover this with a layer of cake, and place in a glass dish. Now mix a **little light sweet wine** with **brandy and water** and spoon it gently over the cake until all the liquid is absorbed. Cover with blanched finely cut almonds. Fill the dish with soft **custard**.

~ Mrs. Clarke's Cookery Book, Toronto, 1883

GERMAN WINE SOUP

Beat **3 eggs** together with a little **flour, sugar** to taste and **1 tsp. lemon juice**. Place in pot with **3 cups white wine** and **1 cup of water**. Whisk till it boils, remove from stove, beat once more and serve.

~ The Royal Victoria Cook Book, Barrie, Ont., 1900

Authors' note: This soup is an acquired taste. It is much improved by substituting **3 cups chicken stock** for the water. Serves 6.

A TEETOTALLER'S CHRISTMAS PUDDING

Put **2½ lbs. flour** in a large pan and add **2 lbs.** stoned Valentia plums, 1 lb. dried currants, 2 lbs. chopped beef suet, ½ lb. brown sugar, 6 oz. candied peel, cut thin, and **1 tbsp. salt**. Mix them well together, while dry. Beat up **6 eggs** in a large basin and add **1 pint milk**, stirring all the time. Make a well in the middle of the dry ingredients and pour in the milk and eggs, stirring constantly until all ingredients are thoroughly mixed. Add **1 pint milk** slowly and continue to stir. The batter should be rather stiff. Have a good stout cloth ready. Wet and flour it well, lay it over a pan, pour in the batter and tie firmly up. When the water in the copper boils, put the pudding in and let it boil gently for 5 or 6 hours. Turn it carefully out of the cloth. Serve with or without sauce.

~ Mrs. Clarke's Cookery Book, Toronto, 1883

Authors' note: We prefer a tippler's pudding.

In the neighbourhood where I was born every man was more or less drunk every pay night. It is by no means the wish of the drinkers that ought to be most carefully considered. There are wives and children. They have the same right to protection from starvation and demoralization that they have from being beaten to death, and they were then not so protected. Many a night I went to bed without any supper because the saloonkeeper had all my father's wages. I know what I am talking about and so do others of my generation.

Tappen Adney, the Maritimer who was sent to cover the Klondike gold rush by Harper's Illustrated Weekly, reported on that most native of all Canadian drinks, Yukon "hootch", as it was manufactured in 1897-98:

Whenever whisky runs short the Yukoner falls back upon a villainous decoction made of sour dough, or dough and brown sugar, or sugar alone, and known as "hootchinoo," or "hootch". The still is made of coal-oil cans, the worm of pieces of India-rubber boot-tops cemented together. This crude still is heated over an ordinary Yukon stove. The liquor obtained is clear white, and is flavoured with blueberries or dried peaches, to suit the taste. It must be very bad, for its manufacture is forbidden by law; they say it will drive a man crazy; but there were persons willing to take their oath that the regular whiskey sold over some of the bars was worse than "hootch." A home-brewed beer, or ale, was also served, a whiskey glassful costing fifty cents. Cigars were mostly a poor five-cent grade.

By 1895 the growing Temperance movement had pacified such hard-drinking towns as Toronto. The notorious Toronto Sunday, drinkless and joyless, was already an established Canadian institution, as Douglas Sladen discovered:

Toronto is one of the most unpleasantly righteous cities I was ever caught in on a Sunday. Tramways do not run, and the public-houses are closed from seven on Saturday night till Monday morning – not that that makes much difference in Canada, where prohibitionist laws are strict, but not strictly regarded. I had this very amusingly brought home to me. I was being driven about the city by one of the leading editors, who was doing the honours of the place, introducing me to all the leading citizens and institutions. Among other places, we happened on the Toronto Fair or Exhibition, where I was introduced at once to the head, who behaved most mysteriously. He led the way straight into his office cupboard, which had fortunately a ray of light, though it was devoted to brooms and such-like, till there was hardly room to stand. It was all about a bottle of *rye*, as they call whisky in Canada, deftly hidden among these Lares and Penates. The exhibition was run on prohibitionist lines weekdays as well as Sundays (though they do not reckon cider alcoholic), and even in the seclusion of his own office the head dared not offer me a drink till he had hidden me in the broom closet.

After the turn of the century, laws against drink grew stiffer. In many areas local option votes forced the hotels to shut down their bars with a resultant increase in the price of food and a resultant loss in quality of cuisine. Frank Leavens, then editor of the Bolton Enterprise, wrote about local option in his small Ontario village, circa 1906:

Our town gets along fairly well since local option, but not so much stir around the hotels as used to be. The bill of fare is higher, but no one can blame the hotel keepers for raising the price of meals from twenty-five to thirty-five and forty cents, for a hungry man will eat ten cents worth of meat alone, besides other things. We don't mean to say that a Scotchman would eat that much, for he would sometimes prefer a good plate of porridge or a good supply of "s-gadden" (herring) and potatoes, but even potatoes run high at the present time, and if a man would or could eat a quart of potatoes and three herrings – let us see, three into twenty-five, eight times and one over, or eight and a quarter cents for herring and five cents worth of potatoes, thirteen and a quarter cents for potatoes and herring. And how much for all the other finery – bread two cents, pudding three cents, cake five cents, tea two cents, sugar one cent, cream (if any) two cents, one quarter of a fruit pie, three cents, making a total of thirty-one and a quarter cents. Allowing five cents for preparing the food for each person, that will make thirty-six and a quarter cents.

So we see there isn't much profit in selling meals, as there was in selling the good old glass, as some term it with sorrow; for when six or eight or more thirsty old chaps (for sometimes they are the worst) would meet at the old familiar hotels, Sandy would treat first. Be Jabers, says Pat, this is my trate. Coom, says George, this is my treat. By Jimmy, I wish not to be behint, says another countryman, we'll have beer. Aye, Aye, says old John, we'll hae a gude glass of auld rye the noo. So when all is done the majority of the crowd are full. Fifty cents would buy all they drank and the hotel keeper got – eight by forty – $3.20, making a clear profit for the landlord of $2.70. No wonder they feel blue!"

In 1910 Msgr. Tauchet ended the Great Temperance Congress, which had been held under the patronage of the Catholic Social Action Committee of the Quebec Diocese, with these wise words. Would they had been uttered half a century before!

"Gentlemen, you are closing a temperance congress. Temperance is not abstinence, fortunately. If temperance were abstinence, the role of the preacher who is familiar with the Holy Scripture would be untenable. Nothing, indeed is so cursed therein as wine: and nothing is so extolled. Wine, gentlemen, is like gold, good or bad. The reasonable quest for gold is useful; the frenzy for gold nefarious. The moderate use of wine is licit; the immoderate use of wine forbidden."

A New Brunswick Smuggling Song

Oh, roll me over a barrel of rum

And I'll roll you a barrel of oil;

We'll laugh in our sleeve as they

    take their leave

And depart from their native soil.

Let prohibition and customs laws

Essay our spirits to damp

We'll drink success to the good old cause

By the light of a kerosene lamp.

~ Published in the St. Croix, N.B., **Courier**
   on Christmas Eve, 1891, and inspired by the
   illicit entry of liquor into Calais, Maine,
   from St. Stephen, N.B., and the flow of
   kerosene in the opposite direction.

A Victorian Drinking Song

Drink to the Queen, my boys, drink!

Our hearts are as full as our glasses.

Who from the challenge will shrink?

'Tis a toast that all others surpasses.

Then drink to the Queen, my boys, drink.

Your hearts in your glasses caress her;

Drink to the Queen, my boys, drink.

Here's health and long life and God bless her.

Cold Water Glee

O come with me and sing with glee,
    Each temperance son and daughter,
A happy band, joined hand in hand,
    In praise of pure, cold water.

REFRAIN
    Cold water, pure, cold water free,
    The drink for you, the drink for me,
    O shun the cup, O shun the bowl,
    It kills the body, kills the soul. . . .

From the Bright Crystal Fountain

From the bright crystal fountain
    That flows in beauty free,
From shady hill and mountain
    Fill high the cup for me!
Sing of the sparkling waters,
    Sing of the cooling spring;
Let Freedom's sons and daughters
    Their joyous tribute bring.

Save the Fallen

Lord before thy holy altar,
    Now thy blessing we implore;
Grant we may not faint or falter,
    'Till our glorious work is o'er.
Saviour! help us; we are trying
    Souls immortal to reclaim,
Thro' intemperance they are dying,
    Snatch them from its burning flame.

CHO. — Save the fallen, make them sober;
    May they feel their sins forgiven.

When this transient life is over,
Give them, Lord, a place in Heaven. . . .

BEER AS A BASE

1867 1967

Canadian beer and ale is rightly renowned, whether it's drunk by the yard, as in the tall glass at the left, or simply from the neck of the bottle. Few Canadians, however, realize that it makes an intriguing base for dozens of soups, casseroles, desserts and punches, a few of which are shown and described here.

BEER SOUP: Beat *1 egg yolk, 1 tsp. flour, ½ tsp. salt, a dash of cayenne pepper* and *1 cup sour cream* together in a bowl. Pour *6 cups beer* into a saucepan and bring it to a boil. Add the beer to the sour cream mixture, stirring continually to prevent curdling. Reheat but do not boil. Place a slice of *garlic toast* on each bowl of soup and sprinkle well with grated *Gruyère cheese*. (*An acquired taste*)

BEER CHIFFON PIE: Soften in water *1 envelope unflavoured gelatine*. Beat *3 egg yolks* and gradually add to them *6 tbsps. sugar* and *1 cup beer*. Now stir in the gelatine until dissolved. Cool the mixture until it begins to thicken. Fold in *1 cup heavy whipped cream*. Pour into an 8-inch baked pastry or crumb shell and decorate with whipped cream, berries or shaved chocolate.

BEER NOG: Pour *1 bottle of beer* into a saucepan. Add a *dash of vanilla*, some *nutmeg* and *1 beaten egg*. Whisk until it comes to a boil and serve.

CARBONADE FLAMANDE FOR SIX: Brown *6 12-oz. slices of ¾ inch rump steak* in a frying pan. In a large pan melt *2 oz. butter* and *2 oz. cooking oil*. Line the bottom with *sliced onions*. Place the steaks on the bed of onions and then cover with more sliced onions. You will need about four pounds in all. Add *2 oz. tomato paste, 2 oz. brandy* and *2 bottles of heavy beer*. Add water to top of pan plus *1 oz. beef base*. Make a *bouquet garni* with *parsley, thyme* and *bay leaves* tied together with a string and add. Bring to a boil on top of the stove, then bake in a 500° oven for 15 minutes. Lower heat to 250° and cook for an hour and a half. To serve: place in an oblong casserole, cover with the gravy and spread with grated *Parmesan cheese*. Brown under broiler and serve with mashed potato and red cabbage. Spare the salt. It's already well-seasoned.

SHANDY GAFF: Mix *beer* and *ginger beer*, well-chilled, half and half.

Photographed at Julie's Place, Toronto.

LEFT BARREL: Beer soup   **RIGHT BARREL**: Beer chiffon pie

LOWER BARREL: carbonade flamande, beer nog, shandy gaff.

5/The Age of Abundance

"Your Paper, Ma'am"
from Toronto Saturday Night, *December, 1887*

In May of 1907, *The Canadian Courier* cluck-clucked editorially over the plight of the Prime Minister who, during the course of a colonial conference, was subjected twice daily to those gargantuan repasts, some of them fourteen courses in length, which the world had already dubbed "Edwardian".

"As Canadians read of turtle soup, *pâté de foie gras* and barons of beef, which the colonial premiers are consuming, the Conservatives chuckle and the Reformers look grave," the *Courier* wrote. "If Sir Wilfrid Laurier should return to Canada with chronic dyspepsia, all the statesmanship in the world will not keep his ways sunny. . . ."

Not only in Edwardian England, but also in colonial Canada, the fourteen-course banquet, lasting from seven until midnight, had come into vogue. The *New Cook Book*, edited by *Toronto Saturday Night*'s columnist Grace E. Denison, laid down, in 1906, the order of such a sumptuous meal, course by course: "1. Shell fish – small clams or oysters, one half dozen for each person, laid in their shells on a bed of finely crushed ice. With these are offered red and black pepper, grated horseradish, small thin slices of buttered brown bread or tiny crisp biscuits and quarters of lemon. 2. Soup. 3. A course of hors d'oeuvres, such as radishes, celery, olives and salted almonds. 4. Fish, with potatoes and cucumbers, the latter dressed with oil and vinegar. 5. Mushrooms or sweetbreads. 6. Asparagus or artichokes. 7. Spring lamb or roast with a green vegetable. 8. Roman punch. 9. Game with salad. 10. A second entrée. 11. A rich pudding. 12. A frozen sweet. 13. Fresh and crystallized fruit and bonbons. 14. Coffee and liqueurs." For such a meal the mandatory dress was white tie and tails for the men, decolleté for the women "the hair elaborately dressed, the jewels advantageously utilized."

Thus, by the century's turn, eating habits had acquired a sophistication unknown in pioneer times. But in the west, coarser provender prevailed as this description of a Manitoba farm dinner, *circa* 1911, suggests:

"Dinner consisted of fried bacon for the second time that day – it is the staple food on most farms – and we had milk-pudding for 'dessert', as Canadians call the second course. Tea, as is the custom throughout the Dominion, was served at every meal, and at first I got very tired of it, and used to supply myself with hot water from the stove close at hand, to the surprise of the others. . . ."

The writer is Ella C. Sykes, the genteel author of *Through Persia on a Side-Saddle*, one of those late Victorian travel writers who, in the interests of authenticity, had decided to rough it on a Canadian farm as "home help". Mrs. Sykes had little trouble since servants by now were in heavy demand and not easy to keep. The governor-general's wife, Lady Aberdeen, writes of almost losing her French chef, Gouffé, because "the ways and manners were rough and . . . the provisions not so good" and he felt he would lose his reputation. In 1894, at Lake Louise, she noted that "servants cost twenty dollars a month and people cannot afford them and if they do get them they marry immediately." A few years earlier, a *Saturday Night* gossip columnist reported that a colonel's wife had actually committed suicide because of her worries with servants and that "everywhere we go we hear complaints of incompetence and utter want of conscience on the part of domestics."

When people start losing sleep over the servant problem it is a sign that the society is an abundant one. From Cape Breton to Vancouver Island, *fin de siècle* Canadians contrived to eat heartily. Effie Bignell, recalling a summer spent in Ste. Anne des Monts, Quebec, before the first war, wrote that "in our menu figure soups of unrivalled excellence; salmon as rich as butter; cod that fairly melts in one's mouth; haddock with all the freshness of the sea's

finest flavour; delicious smelts, herrings, lobsters and all the other fish yields of the generous St. Lawrence . . . Of meats we have . . . such delicacies as beef tongues and sweetbreads. An unlimited supply of the best of butter is at our disposal and a generous allowance of sweet cream figures daily in our menu. The milk and egg supplies appear to be inexhaustible." And she went on with an equally enthusiastic description of breads, berries, fruits and vegetables. At about the same time Laura Beatrice Berton, a young kindergarten teacher from Toronto, was sampling the fare in a Yukon roadhouse – "a long table absolutely jammed with hot food – roast moose, caribou, mountain sheep, native blueberry pie and huge dishes of baked beans." In Montreal, long before this, the ubiquitous Douglas Sladen had discovered that, thanks to the new electric telephones, some twenty to thirty people could be summoned up within half an hour to meet him for tea "with every kind of luxurious sweetmeat and confection sent in as they were arriving." The day of the personal caterer had dawned.

Afternoon tea, indeed, had become the accepted means of social intercourse. Edward Harris in *The Making of a Nation*, written in 1907, called the custom "a marvellous institution" and reported that new members of society could thus fulfil their obligations for about five cents a head since "wine and intoxicants in any form are not looked for in any ordinary home, nor luxuries of any expensive kind." This was not entirely true if we are to believe the social columns of *Toronto Saturday Night*, which, well before the new century's arrival, gave some hint of the elaborate nature of certain teas when it wrote that "few women in Toronto understand the use of the word 'informally'. You are asked to tea informally and on arriving find the street blocked with carriages, the hall, stairways and drawing rooms packed, and about half a dozen women assist-

ing the hostess to receive in low-necked and short-sleeved gowns that would look well at the opera." So-called informal luncheons could be equally luxurious: "You are asked to luncheon informally and find the waiters as busy as beavers attending to about forty people and you leave about in time for dinner with your appetite spoiled for twenty-four hours."

Such ostentation was abetted by thirty years of deflation. Though wages were slightly up, such staples as pork, coffee and rice had not risen in price for a quarter of a century. Flour in 1898 sold for half the 1872 price. Beans and lard had similarly decreased. And unfamiliar new foods were coming in: The banana was still such a novelty in 1895 that the *Ladies' Journal* advised that "this fruit should not be given at all to young children. It should be thoroughly masticated."

There was another novelty, which surely signalled a coming change in the Canadian attitude to food. A new college course known as "domestic science" was already attracting women students. The shape of the future was delineated in 1909 by the principal of Annesley Hall, the women's residence of Victoria College, Toronto, when, discussing the new age of scientific inquiry, she said:

"Should not the same intellectual zeal be competent utterly to burn up and consume the weariness which otherwise attends the creation of those lesser works of art . . . which proceed from the kitchen oven. . . ? Then in that glorious day which is to be, the cook in the kitchen, standing over her scientific cooking stove, the maid in the garden, hanging out her scientifically laundered clothes, the queen in the parlour, testing scientific honey, each and all in their vocations supreme, will be unconscious of and indifferent to heat and blackbirds and sticky aprons: household science will have healed all the present petty miseries of the housekeeper's life!"

SOUFFLE OF CHICKEN

Pound ¼ lb. cooked breast of chicken, chopped, add yolks of 3 eggs, 1 tbsp. parsley, chopped fine, and 1 tbsp. chives, chopped fine. Mix well and add salt, pepper and cayenne to taste. Add ⅓ pint whipped cream and, just at the last, the whites of 4 eggs, beaten to a froth. Cook in soufflé dish for 40 minutes at 325°.

~ The Royal Victoria Cook Book, Barrie, Ont., 1900

KLONDIKE CHEESE

Mix together 1 cup grated cheese, 1 tbsp. butter, 2 tsps. mustard, 4 tbsps. cream, pinch cayenne, salt to taste and bring to a boil. Add 2 eggs, well beaten, and cook without further boiling until the mixture is thick. This is delicious with crackers or bread and butter and will keep for 2 or 3 weeks.

~ The Home Journal, Toronto, November, 1907

In 1886, as a kind of prelude to the age of abundance, an old Torontonian, Conyngham Crawford Taylor, described a magnificent state dinner held at Government House to mark the opening of the Ontario legislature – a dinner, he said, "which eclipsed anything hitherto attempted":

The table was a perfect gem in the way of decoration and arrangement. It was laid in the ball room with covers for fifty-six. Mrs. Robinson herself designed and superintended the work. The centre piece was a miniature lake, in which fragrant flowers of rare delicacy and hue floated amidst tender green vines and lovely leaves, being refreshed by a gentle spray from a rockery, surmounted by a device in which the word "Ontario" glittered in gas. The lake was flanked by a profusion of flowers, and numerous little ornaments and devices added to the beauty and effect of the display, the *tout ensemble*, under a brilliant flood of light, being really magnificent.

In "Arcadian Adventures with the Idle Rich", Stephen Leacock spoofed the "simple" Edwardian life, which was becoming common to the upper classes of colonial Canada:

Life at Castel Casteggio, as the Newberrys loved to explain, was conducted on the very simplest plan. Early breakfast, country fashion, at nine o'clock; after that nothing to eat till lunch, unless one cared to have lemonade or bottled ale sent out with a biscuit or a macaroon to the tennis court. Lunch itself was a perfectly plain midday meal, lasting till about 1:30, and consisting simply of cold meats (say four kinds) and salads, with perhaps a made dish or two, and, for anybody who cared for it, a hot steak or a chop, or both. After that one had coffee and cigarettes in the shade of the piazza and waited for afternoon tea. This latter was served at a wicker table in any part of the grounds that the gardener was not at that moment clipping, trimming, or otherwise using. Afternoon tea being over, one rested or walked on the lawn till it was time to dress for dinner.

In July of 1898, the first two women tourists arrived at Dawson City, on the Klondike, in the heyday of the gold rush. One was Mrs. Mary E. Hitchcock, widow of a U.S. admiral. Her companion was Miss Edith Van Buren, niece of a former U.S. President. Here, Mrs. Hitchcock describes the meal they prepared for Big Alex McDonald, the so-called King of the Klondike. It was served in a giant marquee tent on the banks of the Yukon river:

So the zither was brought out and enjoyed until it was time to prepare the dinner to which we had invited Big A. He arrived at six o'clock instead of seven which we accepted as a pleasant compliment. Isaacs not only cooked, but served the meal as well as anyone at home could have done. Our menu consisted of our last tin of mock turtle soup, which was so greatly appreciated that we were fully repaid for having used it; lobster à la Newburg – the name of which Jones asked many times; E, who prepared it, was flattered by having each one ask for it twice, even though it was made of tinned lobster and California cooking sherry. Next came the leg of mutton which had been hung so long that it was as sweet and tender as lamb, potato balls made from desiccated potatoes, E's famous escalloped tomatoes, my asparagus salad, my peach ice-cream and E's black coffee, with Cresta Blanca during the dinner, "topping off" with a glass of curacoa.

In spite of the new sophistication, bees of various kinds still formed an integral part of rural social life. The paring bee was still an ordinary occurrence each autumn. The softer apples, which would not keep over the winter, were retained by being pared and dried for use after the hardier varieties were gone. These dried apples formed a staple diet among Canadians, especially on the prairies, in the north and in the lumber camps. Here, Thomas Conant describes a paring bee in rural Ontario, circa 1898:

There is much fun and jollity at these bees. After the apples are gathered in the fall, and sweet cider has been pressed out, one of the householders of a group will send out invitations for a paring bee. These invitations are invariably given verbally, and extend to all young lads and lasses, as well as to the married people in the vicinity, not forgetting the school-master. On the night appointed, those living at greater distances come in carriages, but never on horseback; the nearer ones on foot. Horses are put away, and all gather in the kitchen. This is generally one of the largest rooms in the farmhouse, and for this occasion it has been cleared of its every-day impedimenta, and a long table placed in the middle of the room.

The young men do the paring with paring machines. This machine as at first used, before the patented iron article came into use, was of home construction. It consisted of a wooden pulley, about eight inches in diameter, over which a belt ran on a smaller pulley of about three inches. By turning the large pulley great speed was given to the smaller one, to which the fork for holding the apple was attached. The knife for the paring of the apple was held in the hand of the operator. Some of the young men became very skilful in manipulating the knife, and their reputation kept them in requisition at every bee. It is almost incredible how quick one of these experts was at paring an apple. With his home-made machine he could very quickly empty a bushel basket as he deftly and smoothly divested the apples of their skins.

Three or four parers were usually employed during the evening. Along the table the young lasses were seated, and before them were heaped the pared fruit. As a division of labour, the first in order only quartered the apples, and pushed them on to her next neighbour, who, in turn, did the coring; and thus many bushels were pared, quartered and cored in the one evening. They were then strung upon linen thread by the younger persons of the party, who were not supposed to be sufficiently skilful to pare, quarter or core the fruit. Long darning needles with strong linen thread, cut in long lengths, were used. These were driven through the apple quarters, and a string so formed. It did not usually take long for the lads and lasses to be promiscuously intermixed, for no Quaker-meeting formality was permitted at a paring bee. . . .

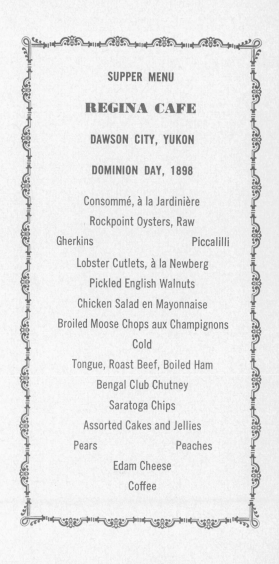

SUPPER MENU

REGINA CAFE

DAWSON CITY, YUKON

DOMINION DAY, 1898

Consommé, à la Jardinière

Rockpoint Oysters, Raw

Gherkins   Piccalilli

Lobster Cutlets, à la Newberg

Pickled English Walnuts

Chicken Salad en Mayonnaise

Broiled Moose Chops aux Champignons

Cold

Tongue, Roast Beef, Boiled Ham

Bengal Club Chutney

Saratoga Chips

Assorted Cakes and Jellies

Pears   Peaches

Edam Cheese

Coffee

*Recipes adapted from
The Royal Victoria Cook Book,
compiled by the Ladies' Auxiliary
to the Royal Victoria Hospital,
Barrie, Ont., 1900*

KROMESKIES

Blanch **3 dozen oysters** and chop into small pieces. Chop an equal quantity of cooked breast of **chicken** with **3 cups mushrooms**, chopped. Make a very thick white sauce using the liquor of the oysters stirred in cream. Add the oysters, meat and mushrooms and the **yolks of 3 eggs** to the sauce. Stir over a low heat for a few minutes. Remove and chill. When cold, mould into cone shapes, roll in egg and cracker crumbs and deep fry.

OYSTER MACARONI

Boil macaroni in a cloth to keep it straight. Put a layer in a casserole, season with **butter, salt** and **pepper**, then add a layer of **oysters**. Alternate until the dish is full. **Mix bread crumbs** with a **beaten egg**, spread over the top and bake.

SPINACH SOUP

Mix together **2 tbsps. butter, 2 heaping tbsps. flour** until smooth. Then add gradually **1 qt. milk, 1 qt. hot water** and season with **salt, pepper** and **nutmeg**. Bring to a boil and add **½ cup cooked spinach**, which has first been rubbed through a fine sieve.

Authors' note: This soup can be served in several interesting ways: with hot croutons cooked in bacon fat or with crisp crumbled bacon or with grated Parmesan or grated cheddar cheese or with sliced hard-boiled eggs. The juice of the spinach may also be added.

MOCK BISQUE SOUP

Bring **1 qt. milk** to the boiling point in a double boiler. Strain **1 pint tomatoes** through a fine sieve and cook in another pan with **2 bay leaves, 2 sprigs parsley** and **2 slices onion**. When the mixture is hot remove the bay leaves, parsley and onion and add **½ tsp. baking soda, 1 tsp. salt** and a dash of **cayenne**. Rub together **2 tbsps. butter** and **2 tbsps. flour** until smooth, add the hot milk, stirring until it thickens, then pour in the seasoned tomato liquid. Stir well together and serve very hot.

It was the duty of the older members of the party to hang the strings of apples, as fast as they were ready, upon poles near the kitchen ceiling. From fifteen to twenty bushels of closely pared, cored and strung apples was not an uncommon result of an evening's work. Thus in a single evening the household was provided with dried fruit for a year's use.

Paring, quartering, coring and stringing at last done, the company rise. A great heap of apple skins, seeds, and cores remain. The next step is to wash the hands in the apple litter, for this is supposed to be a means of preventing the apple juice pressed into the wrinkles of the hands from staining them when they become dry. And so all must thoroughly rub the hands in the apple litter. The lasses scarcely need the caution, for they do not want their hands stained. All "take hold" and clear the room, and in a few minutes it is put to rights, and the company sit upon benches and chairs around the room. The good housewife has prepared her lunch, and each one receives a plate, most likely laden with a slice of pumpkin pie, a bit of cheese and some cakes. Then someone comes around with a pitcher of sweet cider. There is no stint to the amount of food or drink anyone might partake of, and slice after slice of savoury pumpkin pie disappears.

In those days the custom of feeding the local minister by turns was a more widely accepted social practice than it is now. The description of such a meal in Sara Jeannette Duncan's classic Canadian novel "The Imperialist", published in 1904, confirms the suspicion that many a cleric ate better than his parishioners. In this passage, Dr. Drummond, that "tremendous Presbyterian", having managed to arrive for a pastoral visit at five o'clock, allows himself to be persuaded that "on the whole he might manage to stay to tea." Here is the author's description of what that "tea" entailed:

The chicken salad gleamed at one end of the table and the scalloped oysters smoked delicious at the other. Lorne had charge of the cold tongue and Advena was entrusted with the pickled pears. The rest of the family were expected to think about the tea biscuits and the cake, for Lobelia had never yet had a successor that was any hand with company. Mrs. Murchison had enough to do to pour out the tea. It was a table to do anybody credit, with its glossy damask and the old-fashioned silver and best china that Mrs. Murchison had brought as a bride to her housekeeping – for, thank goodness, her mother had known what was what in such matters – a generous attractive table that you took some satisfaction in looking at. Mrs. Murchison came of a family of noted housekeepers; where she got her charm I don't know. Six o'clock tea, and that the last meal in the day, was the rule in Elgin, and a good enough rule for Mrs. Murchison, who had no patience with the innovation of a late dinner recently adopted by some people who could keep neither their servants nor their digestions in consequence.

"Tea", as it was called in the early decades of the century, was a considerably more substantial meal than it is today. But then, in those days, "dinner" was a noon-day meal. Here is a description of a tea served on Prince Edward Island in L. M. Montgomery's "Anne of the Island":

At the tea-table Mrs. Douglas gracefully asked Janet to pour the tea. Janet turned redder than ever but did it. Anne wrote a description of that meal to Stella.

"We had cold tongue and chicken and strawberry preserves, lemon pie and tarts and chocolate cake and raisin cookies and pound cake and fruit cake – and a few other things, including more pie – caramel pie, I think it was. After I had eaten twice as much as was good for me, Mrs. Douglas sighed and said she feared she had nothing to tempt my appetite.

"I'm afraid dear Janet's cooking has spoiled you for any other," she said sweetly. "Of course nobody in Valley Road aspires to rival her. Won't you have another piece of pie, Miss Shirley? You haven't eaten anything."

"Stella, I had eaten a helping of tongue and one of chicken, three biscuits, a generous allowance of preserves, a piece of pie, a tart, and a square of chocolate cake!"

And here, from Evelyn M. Richardson's memoirs of a childhood on Emerald Isle off the Nova Scotia coast, is a description of a noon-time dinner, circa 1912:

And how good those island dinners were! Boiled fish in thick cream-and-butter sauce; leaf lettuce with chopped chives and Mamma's own salad-dressing; new potatoes, peas, beets and carrots from the garden. Grampa's favourite dessert was shipboard plum-duff with molasses sauce, but Gramma insisted upon a variety of puddings and pies. Today, though this was more often a supper dish, there was a huge bowl of the rich pink mixture that resulted when wild strawberries had stood long in sugar and then been added to a bowl of cream for further blending. The cream took the berries' colour and flavour and gave its own in return, so that a dish of this smooth richness bore little resemblance to equally delicious berries freshly sugared and creamed.

In rural Ontario, a few years later, young Harry J. Boyle was enjoying the traditional Sunday dinner that has become legendary in Canada. Years later, after he had become a well-known CBC supervising producer, he set down his memories of one of those meals:

Father flourished the carving knife and stood up in tribute to the brace of plump, golden chickens that exploded with the aroma of onion, sage and marjoram as he cut the strings restraining the dressing. The deep-browned salt pork slices from the breast went to Grandfather who winked. Father nipped off the tail or "Pope's nose", held it aloft, and then skittered it onto the plate of a blushing spinster relative.

The knife flashed as it sliced white meat and dark meat and severed wings and drumsticks to be arranged in remembered choice on

MARROWBALL SOUP

Slowly melt a piece of **marrow**, the size of an egg. When slightly cooled add **1 cup bread crumbs, yolk of 1 egg, salt** and **nutmeg** to taste. Mix well with cold water. Take a teaspoonful and drop into boiling **beef or chicken stock.** Do not cover the soup pot. Should the ball fall apart, more bread crumbs should be added. Put the mixture in by the spoonful and let boil slowly for 3 minutes.

~ The Canadian Family Cookbook by Prominent Canadian Ladies, Toronto, 1914

EGG BALLS
FOR SOUP

Rub the yolks of **4 hard-boiled eggs** with a little melted butter into a paste. Add pepper and salt to taste. Mix in **2 raw eggs,** well beaten, and add enough flour to make the mixture hold together. Make into tiny balls, put into chicken soup or beef broth and let boil 1 minute before serving.

~ Canada's Favorite Cook Book, 1907

Authors' note: Much improved by adding several pinches of **cayenne.**

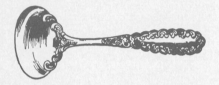

the proffered plates. Mother applied the velvety smooth mashed potatoes with the flecks of green onions and then we had a choice of vegetables. The digestive juices were running madly as the bowls came round. There were slim, tender carrots still tasting faintly of earth, turnips parboiled and then fried in pork gravy, beets hot and tangy of onion and vinegar, parsnips with their exotic, almost perfumed taste, and golden wax beans slathered with little specks of sweet basil.

The sweet butter was sweating at removal from the cool milkhouse. Mother passed the gravy boats, filled with her special pride of blending, gravy and crusty bits of chicken and sweet cream and other odds and ends of kitchen experience. Gravy or butter? Who was to choose? Most of us compromised and used both, smoothing out the mashed potatoes with the butter and then pouring the brown, velvety concoction of gravy over the whole affair.

"Now to work. By George, it looks good."

Someone always made that exclamation. They were always wrong because as if on signal the relishes started coming round. I can still taste those fresh cucumbers, doused overnight in salt and water and then freshened and plunged in salt and pepper and vinegar. The chili sauce smelled of the long simmering of tomatoes, onions and spices that left a day-long aroma in the house at pickling time. Crisp green pickles came with a sweet tang of cinnamon and spice and vinegar from the barrel in the cellar. There were dishes of applesauce and wild crabapples to give a contrast and green tomatoes that could have passed as either pickles or preserves.

Now, it was time to eat! There was a surprise when the flaky, baking powder biscuits with a dusting of flour on top came round to break hotly in your fingers, ready to soak up the butter faster than the knife could spread. The pitchers of cold milk went to the children while the men took tall glasses of buttermilk speckled with tiny blobs of golden butter. Buttermilk, so they said, helped the digestion!

The conversation died away except for a muttered aside and the room was dominated by the clinking of cutlery, grunts and gurgles and an occasional smothered belch. On cue came seconds, and for thirds it was accepted when you steered a biscuit around the plate to sop up the assorted, wonderful juices.

"I'm full. I couldn't eat another thing."

They always said that! They always ate more because the steaming reddish-brown tea helped settle the food and there were pies. Who could resist red raspberries peeking from a latticework of pastry and waiting for gobs of whipped cream, or the spiciness of a pumpkin pie or the seductiveness of apples that were carameled in the crust and made for eating with the tongue-biting tanginess of "rat trap" cheese?

"Aaahhh," someone exclaimed, and there was no need for words; but somehow here and there a diner yielded to the enticement of a dish of preserves. It might be pears tasting of oranges and cloves or peaches in a honeyed syrup. It was natural to have cake with the preserves.

Sunday dinner came gently to an end and as the children fussed at their separate table the men fingered in their pockets for pipes or chewing tobacco. Mother nodded to Father who groaned through the "Thank You Lord. . ." The children bolted for the door and the men shuffled their feet and mumbled praise to Mother and then settled in the shade on the front lawn for conversation and smoking and dozing. The women stayed on to sip tea and talk gentle gossip while their forks traced comfortable abstractions on the tablecloth.

A Quebecker, G. M. Fairchild Jr., set down in 1907 this description of a French-Canadian wedding feast, held at the impossible hour of 7 a.m.:

There was no delay in serving the breakfast and a merrier crowd never gathered at a festive board. The fare, if rude, was generous in quantity. A huge roasted fresh ham graced one end of the table, and at the other a great dish of ragôut divided the honours. There were meat pies, preserve pies, croquignoles, pyramids of hard-boiled eggs, Boswell's bottled beer for the men, and tea for the women and children. A "square-face" of gin was first passed around for *un coup* to the health, prosperity and large family of the young couple, with many sly jokes interposed by all the elders and much laughter from the others.

In "Canada's Favorite Cookbook", published in 1907, Annie R. Gregory, "assisted by one thousand homemakers," described the trend toward the kind of informal supper party which sounds suspiciously like the modern suburban buffet:

The informal, old-fashioned supper, at which all the dishes are placed on the table together, is being revived and bids fair to surpass many of the more sumptuous affairs. People generally are preferring simplicity, and what can be simpler in the way of entertainment than this?

No servant need be in attendance, and as perfect freedom reigns each guest feels free to contribute his mite to the labour of toasting the bread, cutting of cake, carving of meat, and slicing of game, and then too, what a good time everyone has: The host pronounces the word "ready" and brings in a hot pot of coffee with delicious cream, which he, himself, serves, while the hostess loses no opportunity in seeing that everyone is helped to the store of jellies, fruits, and other good things. These indulgent hosts and hostesses make the best parents in the world, and what boy could think of going "out" of a Sunday or holiday night with sociability like this at home? These suppers can take place early in the evening, before church or after. Then comes the singing and the good-byes. God bless such a home.

SOCIAL SPONGES

No. I *"What kind of a house is it?"*

No. II *"O Capital! Best Society. Splendid Girls."*

No. I *"O Hang Society! What kind of suppers, Man?"*

– The Canadian Illustrated News, *January 6, 1883*

In a discussion regarding "food of the Empire" in the September, 1912, issue of the Empire Magazine, Frank Schloesser, describing "colonial gastronomic luxuries – how colonists feed," struggled with the problem of the Canadian cuisine:

When one comes to Canada one is on somewhat delicate ground, for leaving aside the splendid traditions of good French bourgeois cookery in the Province of Quebec, Canadian food may roughly be divided into the rough-and-tumble in the wilds, where, after all, little else could be expected, and the very American food in the towns. Now American cookery is bad from nearly every point of view. It is too elaborate and does not attach enough value to bringing out the true flavour of things; on the contrary, they disguise it with sauces and condiments.

Canadian house and farm cookery is on the whole good, because no attempt is made to make it grand or fashionable, only simple things are attempted, and so success is attained. American "pie" is perhaps too common, for it is indigestible, and unwholesome. But the chickens, joints, and sweets are plainly done as they should be. There is nothing to beat some of the Canadian trout, freshly caught, freshly killed and freshly cooked. The flesh of the fish seems to melt in the mouth with the most delicious of flavours.

A sign of the new times was the subtle appearance of a strange new kind of drink known as the cocktail. It was not to take hold for another generation, but John Kenneth Galbraith, later to become a famous U.S. economist, recalls the early appearance of a cocktail at the legendary McIntyre House in his home county of Elgin, Ontario:

LADY FINGERS

Rub **½ lb. butter** into **1 lb. flour**. To this add **½ lb. sugar**, the juice and grated rind of **1 lemon**, and, lastly, **3 eggs**, the yolks and whites beaten separately and the whites stirred in after all the other ingredients are well mixed together. This dough, if properly made, will be stiff enough to make rolls about the size of a lady's finger; it will spread while in the oven, so that it will be the right size and shape. If you wish them to be specially inviting, dip them in chocolate icing after they are baked.

~ The New Galt Cook Book, Toronto, 1898

O nce a commercial traveller from Toronto had called for a cocktail and gave instructions on how to make it. The patrons were outraged but Johnnie McIntyre quieted them down and went out for ice. This he got from a little iceberg by a tree in the yard. It owed its origins to the dogs who frequented the tree and to the Canadian winter which quickly converted all moisture to ice. Johnnie thought this would return the man to whisky and so did those to whom he quietly confided the stratagem. The man from Toronto praised the flavour and called for another.

In Dawson City, some dozen years after the gold rush had subsided, Laura Beatrice Berton discovered that frontier dining could be just as lavish as, if not more lavish than, the kind she had been accustomed to in Toronto:

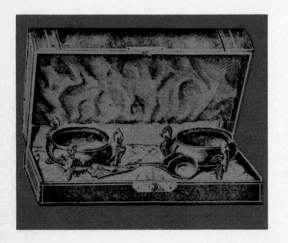

W e sat down at long, polished mahogany or oak tables, covered in net or fine Irish linen, and proceeded through eight-course meals served from Limoges china and accompanied by wines and liqueurs. We went from canapes to clear soup to fish to salad to wild duck to brandy pudding to fruit to nuts. There were always place cards, and specially-made shades for the lamps, and the invariable artificial flowers, in great bouquets at the table, purchased from Turner Townsend (janitor and florist), who in turn bought them from the wholesale milliner-supply companies Outside and fashioned them into exquisite arrangements. After dinner we played auction bridge. There were elaborate prizes: sterling cigarette-cases, good pieces of china, sterling salts and peppers, teaspoons with nugget handles. In short, we lived to the hilt and nothing was too good for us.

Frontier meals of a different sort were described by the redoubtable Ella Sykes who worked as "home help" on a Manitoba farm in order to get "a practical insight into the conditions of life" and to "investigate what openings there might be in the Dominion for educated women." A well-educated, upper-class Englishwoman, she quickly found herself cooking, washing, sweeping and scrubbing:

When these "chores" were done, it was time to peel a bowl of potatoes, the only vegetable used in many parts of Canada, and then I laid the table for the one-o'clock dinner, and put the potatoes on to boil, and began to turn pieces of meat in the frying-pan. Canadians have a perfect horror of meat being "rare", as they call it, and so the steak had to be cooked until it was almost of the consistency of leather. We women waited on the men as soon as they appeared and had taken their seats, and we ate our own meal in the intervals of supplying them with meat, bread, and potatoes, pouring out big cups of tea for them, and dispensing slices of rhubarb-pie. This differs from our English fruit-pies, as the rhubarb, sliced small, is placed on one round of pastry and covered by another, and then baked. Though nice when freshly made, the lower crust soon becomes sodden as the juice oozes through it. Meat and "dessert", which answers to our pudding course, were served on the same plate; but considerate Mrs. Brown produced another one for me, saying "I expect that Miss Sykes is accustomed to have two plates." Of course I declined a privilege shared by none of the family, and indeed, so many ways are there of looking at things, I soon got to approve of the "one-plate" system, as it meant nine plates less to wash up after the meal!

Farm fare on the prairies, though often rough, was generally plentiful – a fact Howard Angus Kennedy made plain in his book "New Canada and the New Canadians" written in 1907 at the height of the great immigration boom in the Canadian west:

The Westerner "lives well." That is to say, he has plenty of good food; but he does not always make the best use of it, and in feeding, if in little else, I should not advise old-country folk to adopt the new-country ways in a hurry. The American, and the Canadian also, generally take too much meat, made as indigestible as possible in the frying pan; and they scarcely draw that distinction between summer and winter diet which the climate suggests. They also take too much tea. I have travelled over the prairie with an old freighter who fed himself – and me, as I remember with pain – at every halt, making five times a day, on fried salt pork, bread, and boiled tea. The western farmer is not a primitive barbarian like that, but he still boils his tea, and the copper-bottomed tea-pot is left simmering indefinitely on the stove for casual use.

As a rule, however, there is plenty of variety in the farmer's bill of fare. He takes porridge and milk for breakfast as well as his fried pork or beef-steak, salt pork being chiefly used in summer and fresh frozen beef in winter. Many of the Americans come in with a habit of taking coffee, but soon fall in with the ways of the country and give it up for tea. Bread making is not as common an art as it should be, and thick bannocks or scones are commonly used when there is no baker within reach. For dinner, besides the regulation meat and potatoes, and bread

Recipes from
The New Galt Cook Book, Revised
Published in Toronto, 1898

SCOTCH POTATO SOUP

Cover **1 lb. pork or mutton**, and **1 ham bone**, with **4 qts. cold water**. Skim well and add **1 onion, 2 grated carrots** and **1 head celery**, cut fine. Slice and parboil **4 potatoes** and add these plus **pepper, salt** and **condiments** to taste. Boil 3 hours.

POTATO PUFFS

Take some **cold beef**, minced fine, season with **pepper** and **salt**. Make some leftover **mashed potatoes** into a paste by adding **1 egg**, well beaten. Roll it out, using a little **flour**. Cut with a saucer, put in some of the meat and fold up and fry in butter or hot fat until a nice brown.

BREAD OMELET

Bring **1 cupful milk** to a boil and pour it over **1 cupful bread crumbs**. Let stand a few minutes. Break **6 eggs** into a bowl and stir, but do not beat, until well mixed. Then add the bread and milk, season with **pepper, salt** and **condiments** and mix all together. Turn into a hot frying pan containing **1 tbsp. butter** boiling hot. Fry slowly and when brown on the bottom cut into squares and turn. Fry to a delicate light brown.

Authors' note: This recipe is enhanced by the addition of **chopped chives, parsley, seasoned salt** and **monosodium glutamate**.

NELLIE'S PUDDING

Mix together **3 oz. flour, ½ lb. molasses, ½ lb. suet**, juice and grated rind of **1 lemon, 3 tbsps. milk, 2 eggs**. Butter a mould and steam 3 hours.

BROWN BETTY PUDDING

Fill a pudding dish with a mixture of one-third **bread crumbs** and two-thirds **apples**, chopped fine. Mix **2 cups brown sugar, ¼ cup butter, 2 tsps. cinnamon, ½ tsp. nutmeg** and spread this mixture over the apples and bread in the dish. Bake very brown.

BERRY DISHES, $3.25 to $10.

and butter and tea, the Canadians, and of course the Americans, will have their round flat pies, containing fruit sandwiched between the upper and under crust – an article known distinctively as American, but exactly similar to the pies I have seen exposed for sale by market women in the old country. There will also be plenty of stewed fruit; either the fresh barrelled apples bought by the well-to-do farmer, or dried apples and apricots, or the small fruits that grow wild almost all over the West, such as strawberries, raspberries, black and red currants, gooseberries, chokecherries, huckleberries, and cranberries. The supper, taken as soon as the day's work is done, is practically a repetition of the breakfast or dinner, with the porridge perhaps left out. Alcoholic drinks are very seldom used or even kept in the house; and, though many a Westerner who abstains at home will not refuse a nip when he goes to town, total abstinence is much more common out there than in the old country. Many Englishmen develop into abstainers when they emigrate; which is just as well, as alcohol has an even speedier and worse effect in the dry western air than it has in the moister atmosphere of the United Kingdom. . . .

A dissenting note came from Thomas William Wilby, another Englishman, who made a motor tour across the country in 1912 and wondered why the Canadian homesteaders didn't take a leaf from the immigrants' book:

Riches in his pocket, but ignorance in his heart and poverty still in his externalities! Poor food, rancid coffee and a hell's own brew called tea, when the same amount of money would buy him the best and a reasonable attention to things culinary would ensure nourishing foods! The peasantry of Europe – the Italian with his good wine, the

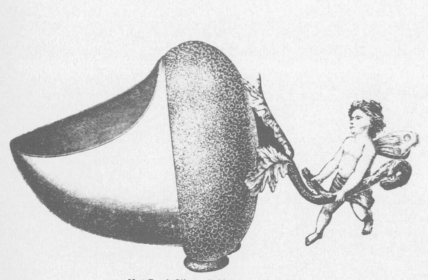

Nut Bowl, Silver, Gold Lining, Value $23.

Grocery department,

74

Hungarian "csikos" of the "puszta" and his goulasch, the German "Landsleute" with their "sauerkraut" and nourishing beer – might teach the homesteader something about kitchen gardens, poultry, and economy combined with good living. I seldom saw a vegetable garden, a flower or a fence in the vicinity of a shanty or farm, and I began to wonder if, in the homesteader's creed, comfort and any attempt at order or beauty were signs of frailty and failure. Was it, conversely, proof of strength and affluence to live on canned foods . . .?

One young immigrant, a Ukrainian named Gus Romaniuk whose family settled in the Interlake region of Manitoba in 1912 in a home of moss-chinked logs, with earthen floor and thatched roof, remembers being ill and contracting a sudden and uncontrollable craving for domestic chicken meat:

I couldn't stand the thought of wild chicken. The fact that there were no domestic chickens in the entire neighbourhood complicated matters. As a substitute, father shot a sparrow. Mother cooked the little bird and also made some sparrow soup, which she placed by my bedside.

Unselfishly, I insisted that the bird be divided into four equal portions; one for each of us children. It made something like a small tidbit of meat apiece . . . My main meal for the next few days was boiled sparrow and sparrow soup. Then father started shooting blackbirds. These were larger and meatier. The soup, too, was more nourishing. And on this strange diet, I gained some strength, although I was still invalided in bed.

Breakfast Castor, Value $9.50

Napkin rings, 75c to $3.00.

T. Eaton Company, Toronto, 1900

THE ABUNDANT BUFFET

Toronto's King Edward Hotel was built just before the turn of the century, and the groaning board shown here is Edwardian in its munificence. In the traditional cold buffet, great roasts and fowls are literally taken apart at the seams and then rebuilt with rich mixtures of meat, truffles and *foie gras*, then glazed and attractively garnished. From left to right, the festive dishes here include *Lobster Pyramid* (the crustaceans are cooked in a court bouillon and decorated with *beurre de Montpelier*), *Pheasant en Volière* (the birds are debreasted and rebuilt with *purée de foie gras* and glazed, then adorned with their own plumage), *Turkey à la Neva* (the breast is removed and sliced and the turkey is filled with *mousse de volaille*, after which the bird is glazed with white *chaudfroid* and then glazed again with pure transparent jelly), two trays of *petits fours glacés* and *French pastries*, then *Restigouche salmon à la Russe* (the fish after being cooked in court bouillon is skinned, decorated with eggs, shrimps, *beurre de Montpelier*, glazed with jelly and garnished) and *Ham au Porto* (the ham is also rebuilt after cooking, glazed and decorated). The basket at table centre is made entirely of spun sugar and behind it is a *Beef Tenderloin Venitienne* (the bridge is cut in one piece from sandwich bread; beef filet, cooked medium and sliced very thinly and evenly, is laid on top of it and decorated with *purée de foie gras*. The tray is filled with jelly to represent a river under the bridge). Such buffets were fairly standard fare at the formal evening parties which preceded World War I. Now they are confined to those luxury hotels whose chefs have the skill and experience to do the job and whose patrons have the expense accounts to foot the considerable bill.

6/The Big Change

The Great North American revolution in eating dates from the early 1920s, when the orange juice mania hit the continent with as much force as mahjongg. Until that moment the consumption of food had been considered, first, a necessity of life and, secondly, a social grace. Since then it has become a good deal more: a craze, a gimmick, a spare-time activity and a concomitant of mass entertainment.

It is not only that we purchase our edibles in a quite different manner than did our forefathers (thanks, initially, to a Canadian named Theodore Pringle Loblaw); it is also that our whole approach to food has undergone a change. There are styles in eating just as there are styles in women's shoes. Breakfast, for instance – that great ornament of Nineteenth Century Canadian society – has become a forgotten meal. Edwardian dinners went out with the Stanley Steamer. Puddings have vanished. Meals grow lighter, courses fewer, quantities smaller. But though we live in terror of the weight charts we have also become a nation of nibblers, gobbling everything from popcorn to cheezies, day and night, in beds, bleachers, orchestra stalls and armchairs.

Since World War I, four major trends have marked the food revolution:

1. *A trend toward informality:* Where are the sit-down dinners of memory – the table crisp with damask and Doulton, the silver aglisten with candlelight, the clear soup, the fish, the roast, salad and sweet following one another in stately procession, the conversation stimulated by good wine and good sauces? Gone, alas, to be replaced by Pyrex casseroles and tossed salads, self-served from buffets and self-toted to rickety card tables or the arms of chairs. How can twenty-two people, distributed variously in den, dining room, parlour and family room, their knees and laps cluttered by

unmanageable crockery, be said to be dining together?

The development of the "cookout" (surely one of the most dreadful words in the contemporary lexicon) is worthy of some applause. In this country, outdoor eating has an honest heritage. A certain amount of charcoal never hurt anybody and the presence of fresh air, as the explorers discovered, is a stimulant. The barbecue also allows people in the subtropical climates of Ontario and Quebec to dress sensibly. Only a privileged minority today is compelled to struggle into a starched straitjacket before nibbling on a morsel of beef.

2. *A trend to expediency.* Nothing is more to be deplored than the tendency of modern hostesses to place speed and ease before quality. Since World War II, dining has been dominated by the lineal descendants of the K-ration. In a country that produces the world's finest fresh meat, we submit to a dozen equivalents of Spam, all of them appalling. We squirt fake whipped cream on our frozen strawberries and douse our instant pancakes with ersatz maple syrup. We drink coffee that has been boiled to a powder and then reconstituted and we kid ourselves that it tastes as good as ever. We allow ourselves to be bamboozled by TV Dinners so lacking in flavour and texture that even Air Canada wouldn't serve them. We order "take-out" food by phone and wolf it out of cardboard containers with paper spoons. We absolutely refuse to squeeze an orange, blithely accepting in its place a variety of beverages, tinned, frozen and crystallized, which, though they all cost more, taste about as much like the real juice as chianti tastes like Chateau Lafitte. When we eat porridge at all, which is almost never, we turn our backs on two centuries of Scottish heritage and settle for something called Quick Oats. Most of the time, however, we prefer Mickey Mouse cereals, crusted

in sugar, with comic-book names. Fish? Our seas, lakes and rivers teem with it but we munch a kind of deep-fried library paste called fish sticks. Bread? We prefer old desk blotters. To make soup these days we just add water and stir and the result, as George Geezle used to say, should better run under bridges. Everything, it seems, is "instant" – from rice to johnny cake. In half our offices lunch comes popping out of a slot machine, wrapped in cellophane and tasting almost as bland. It is a sad paradox that, in the greatest age of leisure in history, most of us won't take the time either to prepare, serve or eat a decent meal.

3. *A trend toward gimmickry.* Food crazes sweep the land as regularly as the monsoons hit Asia. People who wouldn't consider a decent breakfast gobble vitamins by the handful in the belief that they constitute a square meal. We've had a yoghurt craze, a soybean craze, a chlorophyll craze, a pizza craze and a No-Cal craze. The frozen-food people have gimmicked up the dining table with dishes that are often more like kids' toys than meals. The dogfood people have gone so hog wild that poodles often eat better than people. The greatest of all crazes has been the diet madness. Dessert scarcely exists today save, by some wild irrationality, in the form of ice cream, as fattening a dish as was ever set on a table. We eat more ice cream today than we've ever eaten in our lives – in every conceivable form from bonbons to chicken legs. To be fair, the best of it is as good as and perhaps better than the kind churned from old-fashioned freezers. For all the gimmickry isn't bad and some is even sensible, such as the strained baby foods which save so much useless drudgery. But nobody is going to convince the authors that Sugar Jets, Cheez Whiz and Reddi-Whip represent some kind of dazzling gastronomic progress.

4. *A trend toward the exotic.* In spite of what we've said above, it would be foolish to suggest that food isn't infinitely more varied and in many cases infinitely more tasty today for those who will take the trouble to enjoy it. One simple ingredient long understood by the Chinese – monosodium glutamate – has caused a minor revolution in flavour. And, since the end of World War II it has been possible to buy *pure* spices in Canada; before that time the exporters cut them the way dope peddlers cut heroin. The use of herbs has become fashionable and half a dozen useful if gimmicky concoctions, from *bouquet garni* to hickory salt, have enlivened that newest piece of kitchen furniture, the spice shelf. Much of this has been the result of the new immigrant wave. This, along with a new tolerance for wine with meals, has changed our habits and broadened our attitudes. Pizza, chow mein and pastrami may not be terribly exotic or even terribly authentic but they're a step in the right direction. Espresso coffee may have saved the nation, gastronomically speaking. The phrase "gourmet dinner" is perhaps the most overworked cliché in the restaurateur's lexicon but at least it pays lip service to the new thinking that every meal served in a booth doesn't have to be a Greek tragedy. Thanks to the ceaseless propaganda of a small, brave band of extremists Canadians are actually beginning to like their beef rare. Garlic, which used to be a workingman's condiment, is now a status symbol and the occasional pony of wine is being poured into the occasional gravy boat.

There is, then, some hope for the future. It isn't that Canadians aren't eating better than they did in the old days; it isn't that good food isn't available to everyone in quantities and varieties hitherto unobtainable; it's just that most people aren't eating nearly as well or nearly as sensibly as they ought to.

SAUTEED RABBIT

As served in the Mount Royal Hotel, Montreal, on meatless Tuesdays during World War II.

The rabbit should be between three and five months old. Cut it into six or eight pieces with a very sharp knife in order to prevent crushing the bones. Season with salt and pepper and fry in very hot **vegetable oil**. After the meat is well-coloured, drain the fat, add a piece of **butter** in the same pan and let it simmer with fresh **mushrooms** for 5 or 6 minutes. Throw in ½ tsp. **chopped shallot** and ½ **glass white wine**. Add **2 tbsps. rich, thick brown gravy** and **1 tsp. meat extract**. Simmer for 25 minutes, add **chopped parsley** and serve very hot.

For the quarter-century that followed World War I there was scarcely a lyrical word written in this country in praise of food; indeed, there was scarcely a word of any kind written about the subject. The newspapers contained no food columns, and the magazines few food articles. Our novelists and essayists ignored the subject perhaps because the gourmet, in our Puritan scheme of things, was considered something of a sinner. In the following essay, written a few years after World War II, novelist Hugh MacLennan applauds our change of attitude:

A few years ago an article appeared in one of our national magazines which asserted that Canadian cooking, apart from that of Montreal, is the most tasteless in the world and the most carelessly prepared. In a later article in the same magazine statistics were paraded to establish a corollary to the previous hypothesis – namely, that Canadians are the greatest eaters of ketchup known to the Heinz company and that there are many Canadians who eat ketchup three times daily.

The only thing that astonished me about these articles, especially the former one, was the public response they occasioned. The editor was buried under a deluge of letters written by furious housewives and loyal males boasting about their mothers' apple pies. Here, indubitably, was evidence that Canada is in the throes of a moral revolution.

A generation ago most Canadians would have been quietly pleased with a writer who told the world that their food is tasteless and carelessly prepared. Puritanism in Canada was not on the defensive then, and the reading public would have taken "tasteless" to mean "wholesome" and "carelessly prepared" to indicate that we are a people with no nonsense about us, reserving our full energies for things higher than sensual pleasures, of which the pleasures of the table are unquestionably the lowest. Now, it seems, we are almost willing to admit that cooking is an art we may begin to practise one of these days, and that perhaps it might be interesting to climb a few steps up the slippery slope called civilization.

Psychologists have been heard to murmur that the desserts of our childhood are the dishes we most yearn for in our adult lives, and that this is why even middle-aged and elderly Scotchmen continue to eat rice puddings no matter how wealthy they are. If we don't get our childhood desserts, so they say, it is because our wives do not care for them or they have gone out of fashion. But with all respect for my own childhood, which was not an unhappy one, I harbour no nostalgic longings for cold baked-apple or tapioca pudding, one or the other of which invariably made its appearance whenever I visited relations or dined out with a boyhood friend. In our house these were eschewed, at least as a rule, and personally I suffered little from the puritan theory that pleasure in food is a sin. It was the society all around me I am talking about here, not my own home, for the strength of character that made Nova Scotia great was absolutely determined to impress upon children the salutary knowledge that if they really enjoyed what they ate it was probably bad for them, while if they loathed the taste of it, they were being well nourished. So now, as I can no longer postpone answering those letters asking for my favourite menu, I shall do so in detail and with candour.

For breakfast I like a half-partridge *petit pois*, underdone, some light greens and a half-bottle of hock. For lunch I will make do with a small serving of lobster Newburg or a golden-brown *soufflé* high as a chef's cap and enclosing within its airy mystery a nest of softboiled eggs – I ate this once in my life and have never been the same man since. Champagne is a daylight drink with me; I like it best with such a lunch at a table where no politics are discussed. Tea I dispense with unless I am in England, and as I have been in England only for a few weeks in these last many years, let's say I dispense with afternoon tea entirely, for it is poor preparation for the dry sack I like before dinner but almost never drink. Dinner is, of course, the solace of a hard day, and I prefer it accompanied by a variety of wines mostly red, and a really good dinner I like to see articulated with some of the subtlety one looks for, but seldom finds, in a well-worked novel. The oysters should be Malpeques untouched by any sauce, and the meal should continue through vichyssoise on to Dover sole, airborne to Montreal and cooked so lightly I can still taste the North Sea (so subtly different in taste to the western Atlantic) in its incomparable flesh. For the climax to this dinner I should like roast pheasant or woodcock, and before the *demi-tasse* of Turkish coffee prepares my palate for a few dry *fines*, I choose something light, brief and *flambant* for a sweet, followed by a small but knowledgeable morsel of *brie* or of a soft cheese of rare delicacy native to the Ile d'Orleans. Let psychologists make of this what they will.

By 1955, the new approach to eating had become so pronounced that Maclean's Magazine devoted an entire issue to the one subject. In the opening pages, Sidney Katz set out the argument:

. . . It is fairly safe to say that the most fascinating subject in the country today is neither sex nor politics, religion nor women's hats – but eating. A women's magazine recently made this discovery when it tested two different covers of an identical issue. Half the magazines appeared with a cover of a model in an exotic hat. The other half appeared with a cover showing an exotic cake. The cake won hands down, for the issues with this cover far outsold the other.

We have become almost mystical in our approach to eating. Baseball players are apt to explain their batting averages in terms of crunchy breakfast cereals and movie stars their slim hips in terms of patented grape juices. One of the minor deities of the mid-century is a prosperous-looking man named Gayelord Hauser who has succeeded in converting large numbers of people to austere dishes once held to be unpalatable: blackstrap molasses, brewers' yeast, wheat germ and yogurt. The man considered to be the continent's greatest salesman (by other salesmen) is a rotund Texan named Elmer Wheeler whose greatest claim to fame is his "Fat Boy" diet, which has been avidly followed by the readers of 215 newspapers.

For we are as much concerned these days with *not* eating as we are with eating itself. "Calorie" has become as common a word as "vitamin" and metabolism is apt to be discussed whenever four plump businessmen break Vita-Crisp together. Never before have people been so concerned about how much they eat, a fact that may derive from modern insurance tables which show that people who eat too much aren't a very good risk. The newspapers have discovered that diet articles are the greatest circulation builders since the Korean War; family doctors keep printed diet sheets on their desks for their patients; and three out of four supermarkets feature special low-calorie foods.

$1.00

The
Drinking Man's Diet

OR

HOW TO LOSE WEIGHT
WITH A MINIMUM OF
WILL POWER

(ALSO RECOMMENDED FOR
LADIES AND TEETOTALERS)

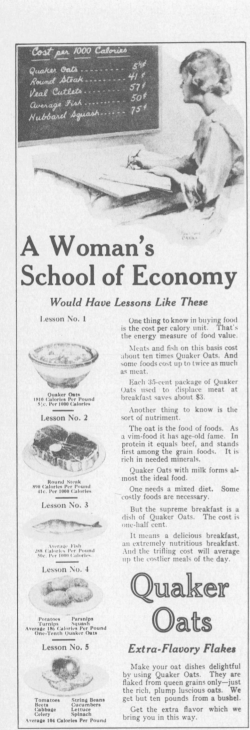

A Woman's School of Economy

Would Have Lessons Like These

Lesson No. 1

One thing to know in buying food is the cost per calory unit. That's the energy measure of food value.

Meats and fish on this basis cost about ten times Quaker Oats. And some foods cost up to twice as much as meat.

Each 35-cent package of Quaker Oats used to displace meat at breakfast saves about $3.

Quaker Oats
1810 Calories Per Pound
5½c. Per 1000 Calories

Lesson No. 2

Another thing to know is the sort of nutriment.

The oat is the food of foods. As a vim-food it has age-old fame. In protein it equals beef, and stands first among the grain foods. It is rich in needed minerals.

Quaker Oats with milk forms almost the ideal food.

One needs a mixed diet. Some costly foods are necessary.

Round Steak
890 Calories Per Pound
41c. Per 1000 Calories

Lesson No. 3

But the supreme breakfast is a dish of Quaker Oats. The cost is one-half cent.

It means a delicious breakfast, an extremely nutritious breakfast. And the trifling cost will average up the costlier meals of the day.

Average Fish
288 Calories Per Pound
50c. Per 1000 Calories.

Lesson No. 4

Quaker Oats

Extra-Flavory Flakes

Potatoes   Parsnips
Turnips   Squash
Average 186 Calories Per Pound
One-Tenth Quaker Oats

Lesson No. 5

Make your oat dishes delightful by using Quaker Oats. They are flaked from queen grains only—just the rich, plump luscious oats. We get but ten pounds from a bushel.

Get the extra flavor which we bring you in this way.

Tomatoes   String Beans
Beets   Cucumbers
Cabbage   Lettuce
Celery   Spinach
Average 104 Calories Per Pound

JAMES BANNERMAN'S FAVOURITE SALAD

Thinly slice **1 orange** and **1 Spanish onion**. Lay in a crescent on a salad plate, each slice separated by a **nasturtium leaf**. Dress simply with **oil**, **vinegar**, **salt** and **pepper**.

There are diets for everyone today: diets that consist almost entirely of fat, diets that consist of *no* fat, diets that require the daily consumption of three filet mignons. Some are excellent; others can be dangerous. . . . But we are rapidly reaching the point where the man with no diet finds himself left out of the conversation.

Meanwhile, writers were beginning to rediscover food as a subject of comment – both critical and lyrical. In his "Diary of Samuel Marchbanks" in the Peterborough Examiner, Robertson Davies eulogized the humble doughnut:

I indulged moderately in doughnuts at lunch today. It is odd that so much has been written about food without any discerning gourmet having paid an adequate tribute to this noble confection. Beautiful to the eye, arresting to the tooth, and ravishing to the palate; fit for the table of a Lucullus, and yet capable of being prepared in the humblest peasant's abode; made from the simplest ingredients and yet a challenge to the art of the subtlest chef; delicious at bedtime and superb in the picnic or "al fresco" repast; adequate to the needs of the famished ploughman yet tempting to the vacillating appetite of the queasy convalescent, the doughnut rises above all common foods with the effortless superiority of a Rhodes Scholar trying the entrance examinations of an Infant Class.

As early as 1939 the Star Weekly reported that the salad bowl had replaced the traditional Welsh rarebit as the pièce de resistance of what it called the Sunday supper treat. In 1951, the urban commentator James Bannerman, himself a one-time apprentice chef, attacked modern salad fetishism:

There are still wistful oldsters who remember when a salad was salad. But that was before scientists discovered, somewhere around 1890, that salad was good for you. The minute this news got out, women who had formerly served salad once in a while because it tasted nice began serving it constantly, just as they would have served stewed cardboard or anything else that had been officially declared good for you. And pretty soon they made a couple of discoveries of their own.

If salad were made to look sufficiently spectacular, no matter how it tasted and even if it had no particular taste at all, it could be used for inspiring in other women a baffled envy gratifying to watch. And with taste subordinated to appearance it could be made of virtually anything – as long as the makings were so dainty and feminine, and so liberally sprinkled with chopped nuts and blobs of marshmallow and such that the salad course got to be a regular nightmare for any man in his right mind.

The decline and fall of salad dates from that discovery, and women are to blame for it; but, in spite of the fearful things women have done to salad, a lot of Canadian men still like it – when they can get it the way they want it, free of gunk and made for taste rather than appearance. Away down in their misguided little hearts, women probably like it that way too.

In the 1950s the critics of Canadian eating habits and Canadian restaurant food were in full cry, as this informal dictionary of euphemisms, compiled by Hugh Garner, the novelist, suggests:

A grill is a room with tables in a hotel basement, where yesterday's dining-room remains become today's businessman's hash. A cafeteria is a chow line where the saving on waitresses is not passed on to the customer. A café is a restaurant with toothpicks on the table. A lunchroom is a counter with stools, carved out of the ladies' wear shop next door. A French buffet is an American invention, at which you try to pile three bucks' worth of food on a plate that holds less than a dollar's worth. A smorgasbörd is a Scandinavian caper to get rid of leftovers when they have no icebox. A lunch wagon is a superannuated streetcar, in which the fry cook hypnotizes you with his skillet gymnastics so that you fail to notice that the chips have been pre-fried and the round steak pounded with a piledriver.

European cuisine means that everybody in the kitchen is an immigrant, and they put garlic in the hamburgers and beets in the soup. A delicatessen lunch is a sandwich bar with dill pickles. A drugstore eatery is dedicated to eating on the fly, but gives the customer a fighting chance for survival by seating him five feet from the bicarbonate of soda. A health bar is a joint where neurotics pretend that carrot juice will replace the martini, and, ambiguously, where they serve nuts with their salads. An espresso bar is where a machine as complicated as Univac grinds, burps and bubbles away, and brings forth a lousy cup of coffee. A tea room is a resting place for varicosed virgins where the creamed potatoes are stamped into forget-me-nots.

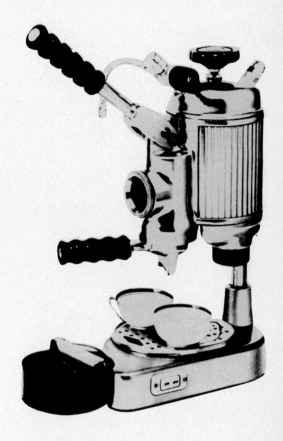

In the drought years, when wine was something fed to skid-row rubbies, the only place you could get a decent meal in many of the smaller cities was the railway hotel. One of the best was Saskatoon's Bessborough, whose maître d'hôtel, Bernard Kluskyens, struggled to bring gracious living to the Prairies – as recounted in this passage by Leslie Hannon:

U nabashed by the fact that most of his fellow citizens prefer well-done beefsteak with French fries to his inspired creations, Kluskyens will zoom into the culinary stratosphere when he wants to flatter an educated palate. He and the chef, Louis Chatvare, may casually produce breast of chicken Eugénie under glass – a triple-threat dish of ham, chicken and rich cream sauce.

Or he may unwind his bolo punch, *côtelettes d'agneau en robe de chambre*: roughly lamb chops in dressing gowns. This is prepared by taking a grilled lamb chop, smothering it with *ragout à la reine* (a cousin to chicken *à la king*), then wrapping the whole in puff pastry to be baked in the oven. This dish was once served to Donald Gordon, the CNR president, and he ate it like a lamb.

Other cosmopolitans who have tested the virtuosity of the Bessborough kitchen range from the world-famous tenor and gourmet Lauritz Melchior and the French diplomat Comte Serge de Fleury to Arthur Treacher, the fastidious English-born comedian, and the indestructible Sally Rand.

This determination to give Saskatoon a cuisine that any Ritz would be proud of wins a curious reaction from the citizenry. They boast

SEVEN HAMBURGER STYLES FOR THE BARBECUE

The BASIC RECIPE contains **1 lb. ground beef, ½ tsp. salt, ¼ tsp. pepper, 1 tsp. onion** finely chopped and **1 pinch garlic salt**. The burgers should be put on the barbecue grid 3 inches above the charcoal briquets and grilled about 15 minutes. Turn only once.

SAVORY BURGERS

Add **¼ tsp. savory** to basic recipe.

PEPPER BURGERS

Soak **4 tsps. pepper flakes** in a little water 5 minutes and add to basic recipe.

SESAME BURGERS

Toast **¼ cup sesame seeds** in a 350° oven 10 to 15 minutes on flat tray. Add to basic recipe.

ORIENTAL BURGERS

Add **¼ tsp. ginger, 1 tsp. grated lemon peel** and **1 tsp. soy sauce** to basic recipe.

DILL BURGERS

Add **½ tsp. crushed dill seed** and **¼ cup chopped olives** or sweet pickles to basic recipe.

HERB BURGERS

Add **¼ tsp. marjoram, ⅛ tsp. thyme, ½ tsp. celery salt,** and **1 tsp. parsley flakes** to basic recipe.

CHILI-CHEESE BURGERS

Add **1 cup grated cheese, ¼ cup milk** and **½ tsp. chili powder** to basic recipe.

~ As prepared at the Calgary Stampede
by the Calgary Rotary Club

about it, but won't eat it themselves. Thus the main dining room occasionally offers the unsuspecting guest one of the few feudal experiences to be found in Canada – the chance to eat alone on sparkling linen in a seventy-five foot panelled chamber under a massive beamed ceiling, with as many as six uniformed servitors awaiting an upraised finger. This can happen any weeknight, while on the ground floor the cheerfully noisy self-serve cafeteria is jammed. During the recent full house for the provincial Liberal convention, the candidates for the vacant leadership and interested cabinet ministers from Ottawa could be seen weaving through the cafeteria crowds bearing loaded trays. The habit is so general that a first-time guest who gets into the elevator and asks to be let off at the dining room will plummet straight to the cafeteria at the street level.

Sometimes, too, some of Bernard Kluskyens's brainstorms backfire. After a formal dinner one night a local businessman phoned the manager, Claude Finlay, and complained of feeling unwell. Finlay asked him what he ate.

The diner admitted to eating quite a bit of "that white balogna". Finlay said he'd check.

Chef Chatvare drew himself up indignantly at the mention of balogna in *his* kitchen. The stuff turned out to be *galantine de capon*, a fearfully rich item compounded of jellied chicken and exotic pastes which, being cooked in a cloth, faintly resembles sausage.

Bit by bit, in the postwar years, the country slowly went wet, with a concomitant improvement in restaurant meals, as one Winnipeg newspaperman, Ralph Hedlin, was able to report in 1961:

Until this fall I seldom dined out in Winnipeg, and when I did I made for a Salisbury House and ordered a nip – which is to say that I went to one of a local chain of all-night short-order stands and ate a good hamburger. Those days are behind both Winnipeg and me. In October I took my wife on a ten-day trencherman's tour of discovery around my own home town. We ate Continental, Oriental and honest home-grown cooking in a score of good restaurants, at least half a dozen of them the equal of the country's best. Winnipeg, we discovered, is suddenly second only to Montreal as a place to eat in Canada – or so say most of the Continental chefs and food-fanciers we met, to our surprise, as we ate our way around town.

We began at Pierre's Café Magnifique, on West Portage Avenue. "How long," I asked when I saw the menu, "has this sort of thing been going on?" "Not long enough," said Maurice Pockett, maître d' and a part owner of the café. He went away with orders for pheasant under glass and Cornish hen, both of them birds not native to Winnipeg until recently.

"This wine would be nice with your dinner," said Pockett, carrying a bottle back with him, and it was. That bottle of wine was a sign and symbol of a happy accident that took place five years ago when the Manitoba Legislature passed a new liquor control act. The legislators are mainly small-town people; some are strong teetotalers and those who aren't feel sinful. They all accept the general principle that food is good, liquor is bad. If they were going to allow liquor to be served at all (and the Winnipeg city slickers had persuaded them that they should) then, by cracky, they were going to make sure that no restaurant would be allowed to serve any more of the sinful stuff than it served of good wholesome food. Dollar for dollar, the food and the liquor accounts had to balance.

The result has been miraculous. Most restaurateurs will tell you they make their money mainly in the bar, but Winnipeg restaurateurs are obliged by law to tempt their customers into spending just as much money on food – otherwise they lose their licences. To sell for that much money, the food had better be good. In Winnipeg, it is.

The two newest crazes – gourmet dining and television – met head on when a Toronto restaurateur, Hans Fread, took to the air with his own cooking show, Hans in the Kitchen, seen on the CBC network. Eric Hutton has described one of its more memorable moments:

By all odds the most unforgettable of Fread's TV half hours was the program that celebrated his fifty-second week on the air. Present was a special audience of semi-celebrities who would be regaled later with the products of Fread's cuisine, augmented by a buffet. Fread's major project was to convert a large leftover turkey into a hot savoury turkey *pâté*, not only to feed the studio audience but for the edification of a home audience plagued by a leftover-turkey problem.

"Of course," said Fread chattily, waving at the array of pots, pans and gadgetry that surrounded him, "you cannot all, alas, have at your disposal such magnificent wares as these the CBC kindly provides for me. Take this machine –" he patted a gleaming porcelain mixer with food chopper attached. "At the flick of a wrist this will produce all the minced turkey we need for our *pâté*." Fread fed several handfuls of turkey into the chopper's maw and turned on the switch. The machine ground doggedly and loudly, but nothing came out. Fread inserted more turkey meat, but still the grinder yielded nothing. Fread rose to the occasion. "You see," he told his home audience brightly, "just like at home – it doesn't work."

Finally he coaxed a small amount of ground turkey meat from the machine, and announced he would make a small "token" *pâté* instead of a large one. With this in the oven Fread gave a sigh of relief and turned to the next item on the menu, cherries jubilee. He assembled the ingredients – ice cream and cherries – and explained that they would be of a quantity sufficient only to be consumed by himself and the program's announcer, Gil Christy. Once more he mentioned the completeness with which the CBC had furnished his kitchen.

"We will now select the correct bowl for our dessert," he said, opening a cupboard door and peering in at the emptiness. Other cupboards proved equally bare. "We will," said Fread decisively, "make our cherries jubilee in a frying pan." Having concocted a tasty-looking dessert in that unorthodox container, Fread reached into a drawer for spoons so that he and Christy could regale themselves. Spoons, alas, were also missing – except for some wooden mixing spoons, which served the purpose, perhaps not quite in the spirit of cherries jubilee's prestige.

As the program moved to its eventful conclusion, the studio audience was torn between admiration for Fread's resourcefulness and fascination at the sight of the first few wisps of smoke curling from the oven where the small turkey *pâté* was all but forgotten. This oversight apparently was noticed by some home viewers, too. Shortly after the program went off the air a viewer in London, Ontario, despatched a frantic wire: "For heaven's sake take that turkey *pâté* out of the oven!"

HANS FREAD'S ADVICE ON BROILING A STEAK

The meat should be well aged. It's a fallacy to think that this means keeping it in the refrigerator for a week. This is not ageing. The only way meat can be aged is in a whole piece. You can't age slices. Prepare the steak by dipping both sides in a good cooking oil permeated with garlic. Let all the surplus oil drip off before putting the steak on the grill. It's important to have a container of water and a whisk handy to put out any flare-up from flaming fats and juices in the fire. When this happens it chars the meat and charred meat is very bitter. The steak should be done on one side and then on the other. A steak should never be turned over more than once. Fire tongs should be used to turn the meat—never a fork. A fork punctures the meat and allows the juices to come out.

A Century of Cookstoves

These ads, from old magazines and catalogues, show that kitchen ranges, like women's hats, can also conform to fashion.

1894: "Rapid" Gas Stoves capable of supporting a wash boiler were advertised in Eaton's Catalogue for $3.75.

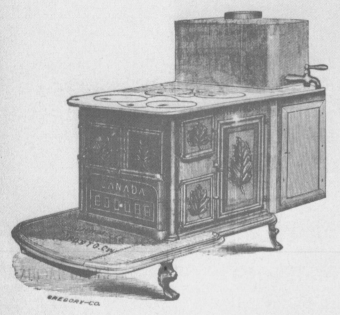

1863: The "Canada" cookstove, invented in Toronto, was advertised as economical, efficient, substantial and neat.

1896: Three-burner coal-oil stoves, like this one, sold for a mere $1.90 just before the turn of the century.

1885: This stove, manufactured in Hamilton, sported an overhead oven as well as a warming tray for coffee jugs.

1901: In Edwardian times, stoves took on a baroque appearance. The Royal Alexandra boasted a "draw out oven plate".

The Etonian Steel Range.

Handsome in appearance, constructed of the very best material, mounted by the most skilled labor, they cannot fail to give complete satisfaction. We may say also that the Etonian is the most economical fuel consumer on the market. The bodies are formed of the very best quality of steel sheets, to which is closely riveted an interlining of asbestos millboard; between main bottom and bottom of stove is a four-inch air space, which protects the floor from over-heating. Add to this a large oven with a perforated loose cast-iron bottom above the sheet-iron oven bottom, also a drop oven door, fitted complete with patent springs, and you have an up-to-date steel range.

No. 0. Etonian, four holes, plain $21.50.

No. 1. Etonian, four holes, reservoir, nickel-plated edges, and ornaments, $30.00.
No. 1½. Etonian, similar to No. 1, but has high warming closet, nicely decorated, $37.50.

The Royal Polished Steel Roaster and Baker.

The Royal Roaster is the latest improved and most perfect utensil of its character on the market. It is unequalled for roasting meats, poultry, game, fish, and for baking bread, biscuits, cake, pudding, etc. The outside pan and cover are made from polished sheet steel, while

1901: Early steel ranges, surprisingly modern in style, vied with the more familiar, ornate cast-iron varieties.

THE COMMODORE

A Beauty in Appearance and Consistently Dependable in Daily Performance

Choice of Coal or Wood Firebox

FOR COAL

65.00
Shipped from Foundry

FOR WOOD

64.50
Shipped from Foundry

A High Quality Range, Built to Give Many Years of Dependable Service

1925: Nickel plating gave the Commodore "a bright, cheerful appearance". And the oven door was of white enamel.

32.95
*

FREIGHT PAID TO YOUR NEAREST STATION IN ONTARIO

STOVES SHIPPED DIRECT FROM FOUNDRY

6 Hole No. 9   32.95

WE WILL REFUND YOUR MONEY IF YOU ARE DISSATISFIED

1913: This is the stove that grandmother cooked on – a genuine Canadian artifact as nostalgic as a farm kitchen.

The CHINOOK

49.50
Delivered

For Wood

52.50
Delivered

The Acme RANGE

1935: These ranges were advertised as being "quite modern in design". You could buy them now in ivory or green.

1940: Early electric range had white enamelled finish.

1966: Some day these will look old-fashioned.

*from the Stampede Barbecue cookbook
of the Calgary Rotary Club*

WESTERN BARBECUED CHUCK STEAK

Sprinkle a **4 to 4½ lb. boneless chuck steak, 2 inches thick,** evenly on all sides with unseasoned meat tenderizer following label directions. With fork, pierce meat at 1-inch intervals to ensure tenderizer's penetration. Let meat stand at room temperature 30 minutes. Meanwhile, make basting sauce: In large skillet, sauté **1 medium onion,** finely chopped, and **1 clove garlic,** finely chopped, in **2 tbsp. olive oil** until golden and tender. Stir in ½ tsp. basil, ½ tsp. hickory salt, ½ tsp. salt, ⅛ tsp. pepper, 1 tsp. sugar, 1-lb. tin tomatoes, undrained, 1 8-oz. tin tomato sauce. Cook, stirring, to boiling point; reduce heat and simmer 10 minutes. Keep warm. For medium-rare steak, broil 3 inches from coals for 20 minutes each side—baste frequently. To serve: slice thinly on diagonal; top each serving with some of the sauce. Serves 6 to 8.

CHUCKWAGON CUBE STEAK QUICKIES

Have your butcher cut thinly sliced cube steaks. Allow 2 steaks per serving. Combine equal parts of **chopped bologna** and **pickle** in a bowl. Spread 2 or 3 tbsps. bologna mixture on each steak. Roll up steaks like jelly rolls and secure with picks. Rub rolls with cooking oil. Arrange fire for grill barbecuing. Place rolls on oiled grid 3 inches above briquets. Barbecue 15 to 20 minutes, turning often to brown evenly.

In the new suburbs, certain native rites, as fixed as the sun dance but all revolving around food, had come into fashion. In her novel "The Torontonians" Phyllis Brett Young described one such ritual: the cook-out:

In a community like Rowanwood you had to ask the neighbours in once a year. It was one of those unwritten laws which, if you had any perception at all, you did not need to have explained to you. It was tribal custom, just as, back in the days on Elmdale Avenue, it had been tribal custom to have at least one really large Sunday tea every winter, with the whole household upset for weeks in advance, and all the best silver and lace brought out, right down to those antique silver teaspoons of your grandmother's that were never used at any other time and were always black with tarnish when found where nobody could ever remember having stored them. . . .

The food you served at a cook-out was relatively simple. It was the quantity you had to handle, and the cost, that threw you. At least that was the way things were in Rowanwood. In Rowanwood you did not offer your guests hot dogs and hamburgers, as you had on Gavin Street, you gave them the best steaks available, together with those special rolls you could get only at the Pâtisserie Française. You also made up enormous amounts of tossed salad, done the way you had learned to do it in Geneva, with leaf lettuce and oil and vinegar. You served mustard and catsup because you knew you had to, but ever since Geneva this had been something it really hurt you to do. And then for dessert you had those marvellous little rum cakes that had to be ordered by mail from that store in Stratford.

You were the only one in Rowanwood who knew about the store in Stratford. In your mother's and your grandmother's day family secrets of this kind consisted of recipes handed down from one generation to another. Now you simply tried, whenever possible, to keep people from knowing where you bought things. Both Betsey and Millicent had, you knew, snooped through the kitchen at last year's cook-out in an effort to find the containers in which the rum cakes had arrived. When you found this out, you didn't feel quite such a fool for having hidden them under the bed in the guest-room. You had reasoned, and correctly, that the sort of person who would be interested in the guest-room bed would not be the sort of person who would care where you bought your rum cakes.

There was no end in sight to the trend towards instant foods. In 1959, the male author of this book made a rueful report to the readers of his newspaper column on the latest scientific developments:

Well, sir, if anybody had told me a fortnight ago that I should shortly sit down to a multi-course meal composed entirely of dehydrated foods and featuring, as a sort of appetizer, a plateful of Instant Spam, I should have called him a blackguard.

All the same, it has happened. Some time ago you'll perhaps recall I wrote a piece about the Just-Add-Water-and-Stir philosophy, in which I smote the jiffy food craze hip and thigh. Since then, I've been waiting for the instant people to strike back. They finally got to me last Thursday.

I tell you without a word of lie that I was served up a meal which included instant fruit juice, instant soup, instant hamburgers, instant roast pork, instant rib steak with instant mashed potatoes and instant peas and carrots, instant pork chops with instant apple sauce, instant chicken *à la king*, and instant fruit jelly.

The deus-ex-machina which brought me an Instant Meal face to face was Mr. Leonard Bertin, the Star's Science Editor. Mr. Bertin's name so closely resembles mine that we keep getting each other's phone calls, and this had led to a rewarding friendship marred only by Mr. Bertin's stubborn addiction to Nescafé.

Mr. Bertin has recently been delving into some interesting experiments conducted by the Department of Defence Research Medical Laboratories at Downsview. As a result of his deliberations, he and two scientists arrived at my place the other night just before the dinner hour with a large cardboard box. Mr. Bertin reached into the box and produced what appeared to be a piece of pink *papier-mâché*.

"This," he said, "is an instant pork chop." And it was.

The scientists with him were Dr. Walter Smithies, chief of the Instant Pork Chop Project at Downsview, and his colleague, Miss Maryl Ballantyne. Miss Ballantyne, I recalled, had mentioned me in a speech about instant foods a day or so before in which she referred to me as a diehard fighting a trend.

Well, I have an open mind about most things, and so, in just about the time it takes to turn on a tap, we were all digging into a full-course Instant Dinner.

I guess this is the strangest meal I've ever eaten. Everything on the menu had had 98 percent of the water removed, so that it was all as light as marshmallow, and as tough as cardboard. Five minutes' soaking rendered it edible. The vegetables and chicken *à la king* were soaked in hot water and served ready to eat. The steaks and chops were soaked in cold water and pan-fried.

I am duty-bound to say that the rib steak was as good as any grilled rib steak in a medium-priced steakhouse, that the pork chops tasted exactly like pork chops anywhere, that the chicken *à la king* was an exact replica of the chicken *à la king* served at Rotary Club luncheons, and the mixed peas and carrots were just like the kind you get in a Greek restaurant.

It occurs to me that all this is a scoop for this column, since very little has been released on the new look in instant foods. Remember: you read it first in this space. The secret is that the foods are first frozen solid and then dehydrated in a vacuum. If you remember your high school physics, you'll recall that water can be boiled in a vacuum without even getting warm. In the same way the water is removed from the frozen foods without the usual hot air that makes them lose their shape.

They did this with penicillin and blood plasma during World War II, and now Dr. Smithies and Miss Ballantyne are using the same system on raw beefsteak and cooked peas. They've made some interesting discoveries. For instance, they've found the system works better on commercial grades of beef, which are tougher. The dehydration process also seems to tenderize, so a good grade or good cut will go mushy. We used Blue Brand rib steak and it was fine, though it took several tries before we could get one rare. The dehydration seems to cook the meat, in a sense, so that it needs only half the normal time in the pan.

Western Barbecue Recipes

from the Stampede Barbecue cookbook of the Calgary Rotary Club

STUFFED WHOLE FISH

Select a firm-fleshed fish weighing about 3 lbs. Have it cleaned and the head removed. Prepare **Rice Stuffing** (see below) and spoon it into fish cavity. Close cavity and head opening by inserting small metal skewers at 1-inch intervals; lace securely with twine. Tie more twine around entire length of fish at ½-inch intervals. Put fish on spit. Arrange hot briquets to give high heat for spit barbecuing. Attach spit to the unit. Put a drip pan under fish; start barbecue—cook fish 15 or 20 minutes or until done, brushing often with oil. Fish is done when it flakes with a fork.

RICE STUFFING

Combine in a bowl ¾ **cup cooked rice, 1 clove garlic**, minced, **3 tbsps. onion**, minced, **¾ tsp. salt,** dash black pepper, ¼ **cup green pepper**, minced, **1 tomato**, peeled and chopped, **1½ tsps. parsley**, chopped. Toss the mix well. This yields about 1½ cups of stuffing.

*Instant coffee advertised
in Eaton's Catalogue
for 1913*

Under this system, food can be either pre-cooked, like our apple sauce, which was whipped up in an instant, or dehydrated in a raw state, like our pork chops. Fat doesn't dehydrate properly, nor do smoked meats, such as pastrami and bacon, nor large roasts or whole chickens. But we had a fruit compote which, after three minutes' soaking, was indistinguishable from the tinned variety.

The implications of all this are obvious, and some of them pretty terrifying. If this stuff goes on to the Loblaw shelves, as I'm sure it will eventually, there will be no reasoning with the women. You can kiss goodbye to corned beef and cabbage, Berton's fresh tomato soup, bacon and eggs, and Morton Bennett's Christmas turkey. It'll be Instant Spam and instant mashed for dinner while the little woman slaves over a hot television set.

On the other hand, these things, which were developed for the armed forces (and have yet to be tested in the field), are certainly a boon to the infantryman. As it has now become impossible to make army food any worse, the defence department, in a remarkable about-face, has turned its talents to making it better. And this stuff certainly *is* better than the swill those blacksmiths served us back in 1943. Also, it's about nine times lighter and, if kept away from the air, will stay

edible practically forever, qualities that make it pretty attractive to campers, fishermen, summer bachelors, bush pilots and Career Women.

As the meal progressed, I wrote down some informative snippets of conversation.

"I had instant wine once. You just added vinegar and stirred. Not too good."

"Dehydrated steaks make the best insulating material in the world."

"We could make instant French peas, too, but the average Canadian wouldn't like them. Anything fancy is out, as far as the forces are concerned."

"The British army has an instant jam."

"We haven't got an instant pastrami yet, but we're working on it."

I asked if they ever got tired of eating instant foods.

"Oh, I'd never eat them myself," said Dr. Smithies. "Actually, this is the first fully instant meal I've ever had."

"Shall we finish with instant coffee?" cried a voice from the kitchen.

There was a sort of embarrassed silence and then I said: "Let's cheat and have the real stuff," and there was an instant sigh of relief all round.

HOW TO MAKE
INSTANT POTATO CAKES

Soak **2 tbsps. instant onion flakes** in **1 cup water** for 5 minutes. Add **¾ tsp. salt** and bring to a boil. Remove from fire and add **¼ cup milk**. Stir in **2 cups instant potato flakes** and **1 tbsp. instant onion juice**. Add **½ tsp. ground black pepper**. Cool. Form into thin patties and fry in an iron pan in bacon fat, turning with a lifter until both sides of each cake are a crisp, golden brown.

This is a basic recipe, to which other ingredients may be added:

For fish cakes add **1 cup tinned salmon** or **1 cup flaked cooked codfish**.

For bacon cakes add **½ cup crumbled crisp bacon**.

For corned beef hash add **1 cup crumbled tinned corned beef**.

For turkey patties add **1 cup finely chopped cooked turkey**.

BEEF ON THE

The barbecue craze, which hit the United States with such force in the post-war years, was late coming to Canada, perhaps because Canadians have always been used to cooking outdoors on various makeshift and unpatented devices. The one shown above was made from granite blocks, bought for fifteen cents apiece from the Toronto Transit Commission, which had used them for decades as paving blocks beneath now-obsolete streetcar tracks. The blocks came to Canada from Scotland as ballast in wheat ships.

The beef is Scottish, too, being the finest Black Angus available, raised on a farm not far from these fields. The cut is not cheap but if you're inviting special guests who enjoy good food, then this is the one for you.

Ask your butcher for a rolled porterhouse roast with the tenderloin removed (otherwise it will be too unwieldy for the spit). The resultant roll of meat should weigh about ten pounds. But before he rolls

BARBECUE

the roast, give him the following mixture of ingredients:

1 tbsp. oregano, 1 tbsp. thyme, 1 tbsp. celery seed, 1 tbsp. marjoram, 1 tbsp. minced garlic, ½ tsp. rosemary, 1 tbsp. cracked black pepper and 1 tbsp. salt.

Cover the raw meat with this dark and aromatic powder, as shown above. Then have your butcher roll it tightly and cover with a layer of fat. On a hot barbecue it should not stay on the rotating spit longer than 45 minutes, assuming that you like your meat rare. Certainly, it would be sacrilege to serve this beef well done.

There should be enough here to feed ten hungry trenchermen, allowing a pound per person. It should be sliced with a sharp knife into thick slabs and served either on a plate or directly onto slices of garlic bread. As a side dish the authors usually have a bowlful of fresh spring onions on hand. Nothing else, really, is needed.

7/Wilderness Fare

Illustration from Toronto Saturday Night *for December 1888*

It's not really very surprising that some of the most powerful writing about food in Canada over the past century has actually been about the absence of it. For hunger – gnawing, obsessive, hallucinatory – has been part of the Canadian experience since the time of Champlain. The literature of starvation in Canada is quite as rich as – and often more eloquent than – the literature of gastronomy. After all, a man who has known famine is well equipped to make a bannock sound like a soufflé; indeed, as the authors have discovered, there is an entire enthusiastic sub-literature of the bannock in Canada that deserves the anthologist's attention.

Some of the most typical Canadian meals have been those eaten in circumstances of utter despair and privation. Shoe-leather, it can be argued, is a Distinctive Canadian Dish – a fact readily confirmed by that most memorable of all motion picture sequences in Chaplin's *The Gold Rush*. These scenes were founded on fact: In the fall of 1909 the Bishop of the Yukon, Isaac O. Stringer, and his Anglican missionary companion, C. J. Johnston, lost in the mountain wilderness north of Dawson City, kept body and soul together by feasting on their Eskimo boots. The Bishop's laconic diary of those days has been preserved.

October 17: Travelled fifteen miles, Made supper of toasted rawhide sealskin boots. Palatable. Feel encouraged.

October 18: Travelled all day. Ate more pieces of my sealskin boots boiled and toasted. Used sole first. Set rabbit snares.

October 19: No rabbit in snare. Breakfast and dinner of rawhide boots. Fine. But not enough.

October 20: Breakfast from top of boots. Not as good as sole.

Some of the best meals ever described in this country have been fantasy repasts consumed only in the imagination of shivering men. In August of 1925, John Hornby, the curious northern recluse, and his companion, the pukka sahib James Critchell-Bullock, half-starved and trapped by the shrieking wind on the unmapped tundra west of Aberdeen Lake in the heart of the Northwest Territories, whiled away the time making day-by-day menus of what each would like most at waking, breakfast, *petit déjeuner*, luncheon, tea and dinner. Hornby's biographer, George Whalley, has left us a description of one such hallucinatory meal:

HORNBY

One magnum best Heidseick

Salmon mayonnaise

Egg soufflé

Roast pheasant and chips

Mince pies

Preserved assorted fruits

Ice cream

Cheese

Coffee

Crackers

Hot rolls

BULLOCK

Clover Club cocktail

Old brown sherry

Magnum Charles Mumm

Sweetbread patties

Lobster mayonnaise

Roast dressed pheasant

Mashed potatoes

Best brandy trifle

Assorted crystallized fruits

Ice cream and sponge fingers

Stilton

Turkish coffee

Nuts

Marsala

Yet some very real meals, eaten under the most adverse conditions in odd, uncharted crannies of the land, are enough to make the mouth water. Take, for instance, the unorthodox menu enjoyed in the Kootenay mountains of British Columbia in 1887 by two English explorers, J. A. Lees and W. J. Clutterbuck. Both men arrived at their camp in wretched shape, having scrambled through a fire-ravaged forest "black from head to foot, cut, scratched, bruised, clothes torn, limbs racked, tempers unspeakable and parched with thirst from the fine charcoal dust with which at every movement the air was filled." Suddenly they burst upon a small green plateau and found that their guide had prepared the following menu:

Fish	18 Charr
Entrées	Kidneys, Heart, Liver and Marrow – de Mouton de Montagne
Joint	Biftek du Bighorn Sauvage
	Peasoup

"The memory of the supper we had that night will dwell in our hearts for aye," the pair wrote later in the lyrical fashion of the day.

There are few Canadians who at some time in their lives have not experienced a similar moment of ecstasy, for this is still an outdoor nation of campers where, after a hard climb or a long day on the trail, life is made sweeter by the scent of coffee brewing in the billy, fish sizzling in the skillet or beans bubbling in the pot, the whole suffused and heightened by the incense of woodsmoke and green spruce.

Yet there remain certain distinctive outdoor dishes which few Canadians have experienced. Not many of us have yet had the opportunity afforded Doug Wilkinson, who lived for a year with the Eskimos of Baffin Island and was

able, as a result, to compile a list of his favourite Arctic dishes, in descending order:

1 Raw frozen caribou meat eaten with chunks of back fat; meat thawed just enough to be crunchy.

2 Boiled muktuk and whale heart, done together in the same pot.

3 Raw frozen square flipper seal intestine, contents squeezed out at time of kill.

4 Raw frozen Arctic char, fish cut in sections, section next to tail most delicious part.

5 Boiled caribou, char, rabbit, ptarmigan, with drink of soup of water used for boiling in each case.

6 Boiled seal meat, the flippers the choice part with ribs close behind.

7 Raw unfrozen meat from young seals in the spring, heart and liver the choice tidbits. Liver has onion taste.

8 Dried strips of whale meat or Arctic char.

Wilkinson adds that his list presupposed that boiling is the only means of cooking, otherwise fried seal liver, fried caribou steak and stuffed roasted baby seal would also be on it. The most adventurous gourmet may shrink from such a primitive menu but it must be remarked that Doug Wilkinson not only thrived for a year on this sort of fare but also actually came to look forward to it: he writes lovingly about raw seal's guts the way some men write about omelettes. For food by definition is a matter of taste and hunger by common agreement is the greatest of all sauces. Which helps explain why some of the tastiest meals ever eaten have been composed of old boot soles, raw fish or simply flour, water, baking powder and salt fried in a glutinous grease.

From *Land of the Long Day* by Doug Wilkinson, published by Clarke, Irwin & Company Limited. Used by permission.

In D. K. Findlay's novel "Northern Affair", about a scientific expedition north of Baffin Island, one of the characters, Dr. Poldar, paints a horrifying picture of what starvation can be like under Arctic winter conditions:

Listen! It will be dark, and with the darkness comes the cold. And the wind. We could not go outside even if there were light; we would become paralyzed by the cold. We would freeze to death because we have not the proper clothing. So we lie in our sleeping bags and wait. The food comes to an end; we eat all the scraps we can find, our boots, bits of leather, cloth with grease on it – anything – because we are starving. It's not an easy death, you know – you cannot sleep because of the pains in your stomach and you come out in sores. Your teeth fall out. You are apt to suffer hallucinations – you may wake up and find yourself eating earth and stones in the delusion that they are meat and bread – or you rush into the sea, believing that you see a ship out there. . . . Dr. Borg knows all about these things, he knows what it's like to be really hungry. Then we'll quarrel, we'll distrust one another and spy on one another in the belief that someone is getting more than his or her share of food – or else someone has a secret hoard of food somewhere and will not share with the others. Perhaps we'll fight – real fights with fists and stones – perhaps the stronger will decide to kill the weaker ones and eat them – it won't matter much then. The end will come for all of us, you will no longer care what happens to you. You will lie in your bag and not care and one day you will not wake up. Then the tent will fall in and the snow will cover it and that will be the end – a row of skeletons under the snow. . . ."

In 1937 a former Mountie and one-time British army riding master, John Stanwell-Fletcher, took his American wife Theodora to a wilderness home in Driftwood Valley, in north-central British Columbia. Their mission was scientific; their aim: adventure and solitude. In the book that resulted from the experience, Mrs. Stanwell-Fletcher described how it felt to go on short rations:

Nothing in the world seemed important any more except food. We had left eight pilot biscuits, enough split-pea powder for four servings of soup, a very little tea and cocoa, but we ate such small quantities at a time that it seemed to me my stomach felt worse after eating than it did before. . . . *So,* this was what it meant to be hungry. And we weren't starving – yet. This was nothing to what J. had experienced in the Arctic when he and an Eskimo were snowbound in an igloo during a terrible storm. They ate their sealskin boots and some of their dogs, and very nearly died before they finally reached home. I understood why men who are really hungry steal and kill, why women sell themselves. *We* had no reason for despair. We expected the plane would come when it cleared; we had other loopholes. But if I were hungrier than this and had no hope, no one to keep up for, I should have no more scruples than the lowest of the low.

In December, 1921, Cyrus Bryant, a settler in the heart of British Columbia's ranching district, decided to move his family from Soda Creek to a new home near Tatla Lake. Off they set, in two wagons and a buckboard, with their four children, twelve head of cattle and all their worldly goods. At Sawmill Creek the snow was falling so heavily it smashed their tent pole. His wife Phyllis described the meal they ate outdoors the following day:

Packing up next morning in the deep snow was something I don't like to remember, but by daybreak the wagons were loaded. The horses strained in the traces and we moved off, slowly through the untracked snow. It was much colder now – perhaps thirty below by the time we stopped for lunch. Before beginning the journey I had made a boiler full of chili con carne and added cooked macaroni to the mulligan. With ground meat, beans, tomato soup, and macaroni all in one dish, meals were simple. We just chipped off chunks of the frozen mass, added snow or water, and brought it to a boil. With bread and jam and a mug of hot coffee we had a meal. It gets monotonous perhaps – unless you are hungry.

In his poetic book, "The Wind and the Caribou", Erik Munsterhjelm, a trapper turned writer, told of one hungry moment spent with a companion in one of the great empty areas beyond Lake Athabasca. The year was 1934:

We were now practically without provisions. Except for pancakes and stick bread – strips of dough wound around a stick and baked by an open fire – tea was all we had in the way of food.

And the storm blew unabated. We were only ten miles from the fort, but that did not help us much. It was still blowing the next day, and we hunted for food along the lakeshore and in the surrounding bush. But there was no game now, when we needed some. Our foraging netted us only a jackfish, a fingerling, that made only one bite apiece. There were not even any ducks.

"Oh yes, this is a regular banquet," said August, as, two nights after the mishap, we divided a pancake baked from our last flour. "Won't you have some jam? Here, take some, there is lots more." He offered me the cup with some last year's cranberries, which we had picked on the north slopes of a hill. But we did have tea, which we drank strong and hot.

The next day was dreary. The wind still blew, and the whitecaps still raced over the lake. Three miles away was the south shore, from which we could walk to the fort in two hours. But that thought did not satisfy our complaining stomachs. It was getting dark, and we made ourselves ready for another night with empty stomachs.

"Have you seen Chaplin's Gold Rush, Erik?" he asked.

I looked at him and grinned. "Sure, I remember it. Do I look like a chicken? They ate their shoes first though," I suggested.

"Yes and licked the nails, too," said August, and walked out for a look at the lake.

Then I heard a shout: "Hi, Erik! Come here!"

I rushed out. There August was slamming away with a big stick at something on the ground. A porcupine! God bless all porcupines! In

Lees and Clutterbuck's camp at Sinclair Pass, in the mountains of B.C., 1887

TORTILLA

Make ordinary dough, as for bread. Plant a stick in the ground near the fire at an angle of about 25 or 30 degrees. Have another clean stick ready, and a frying pan of lard or butter heated as hot as possible short of burning it. Take a piece of dough the size of a small hen's egg, flatten it between the hands and making a hole in the centre, quickly work it out into a flat ring of about two inches inside diameter. Drop it flat into the grease (the pan, of course, is kept on the fire), which should easily cover it, turn it almost immediately, and in a few seconds it will be cooked. When of a light brown colour, fish it out with your little stick and hang it on the slanting one. If the grease is the right heat, the cooking of one tortilla will occupy just the same time as the forming of the next, and so the process goes merrily on until the slanting stick is full of lovely crisp crumpety rings, which are hailed with joy by your companions when they come in tired and hungry.

~ "A Ramble in B.C.", 1887, by J. A. Lees and W. J. Clutterbuck

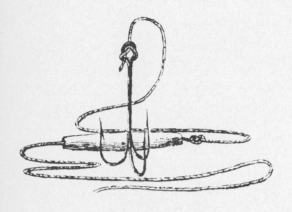

YUKON BUD FISHER'S
WILDERNESS STEW

Cube **2 lbs. lean beef** into a Dutch oven and season with **garlic powder, salt, pepper, 1 pinch nutmeg, 3 pinches thyme, 1 pinch cayenne**. Add **1 package dry onion soup** and **½ cup water**. Cook in the Dutch oven for about half an hour, then add **3 onions, halved, ½ doz. carrots, ½ small turnip, several stalks of celery** cut coarse and cook for one more hour. When cooked, throw in a handful of **egg noodles** and add a little water. Thicken with **rice flour** and reheat. Serves 6 to 8 hungry men.

PIGJEREE

Chop **½ lb. sliced bacon** small and fry it in its own grease until soft. Then stir in **2 cups boiled rice**, season with **salt, pepper** and **curry powder**. Cook until the rice begins to brown stirring occasionally to prevent it sticking.

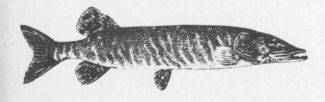

spite of quills and so on we skinned it in record time, and before I had taken out all the innards August had brought the water in the pot to the boil.

"Look how fat it is," he sighed as he grabbed a big piece and sank his teeth into it. We ate the whole thing in one sitting, although it weighed at least eight pounds. It tasted better than tenderloin.

In 1909, Dougall McDougall, son of a Winnipeg broker, described for The Canadian Courier his gastronomic experiences as a member of a party surveying the route of the Grand Trunk Pacific Railway:

At noon our lunch is frozen solid and the noon camping-place takes a lot of labour to prepare. We first cut lots of dry wood and secure birchbark, if possible; then cut brush and carpet the ground to keep our moccasins dry; cut a pole to hang our tea-kettle on and hunt for water. The deep snow keeps the water-holes from freezing, but they are hard to find, and when found the water usually smells pretty bad, but tastes all right in tea. Often as a last resort we use snow. Those times I don't drink tea, for the snow burns, and the tea has a taste very similar to carbolic acid. We place the lunch around the fire until it thaws out, but often a sandwich is burned on one end and still frozen on the other end. I can tolerate frozen cakes or pie, but canned roast beef *frappé* is distinctly unpalatable. After lunch we always enjoy a good smoke around the fire, for in severe weather away from the fire, smoking is a rank failure. Your pipe freezes up between puffs, matches give a feeble blaze, and go out before you can get a light. Even the axes refuse to work; chopping green wood makes the edge bend or chip off, according to the hardness of the metal. Ours looked like tin the other day.

In his book "The Lonely Land" Sigurd F. Olson, perhaps the best-known wilderness writer on the continent, told of one memorable meal at Dipper Lake in the Shield country far to the north of Lake Superior on the old trail of the voyageurs, which he retraced as the leader of a party of six:

Tony and Elliot decided to celebrate by catching fish. In a short time Tony, casting off the rocks with a red-and-white daredevil, had taken thirty-two northern pike and walleyes. He let most of them go. Elliot, standing on a rocky spit above him, caught as many with a red-and-white Bass-oreno. It seemed to make little difference what they used, for the fish struck at anything that looked like food. In half an hour Tony brought me a baker's dozen of walleyes for chowder and fillets.

It seemed good to cook a meal without hurrying. I cleaned and prepared the fish and kept the fire going while absorbing the scene. When the dried potatoes and onions were simmering gently I added the fish, seasoned it with salt and pepper, added a little powdered milk and a spoonful of precious tinned butter. That, I said, was something special for Eric, who needed the additional nourishment. Here was chowder as it is made in the North and as the Finns and Scandinavians have made it for centuries in Europe. No tomatoes, pork or bacon, no fancy ingredients. Just fish, potatoes, and onions, with a little something extra for good luck. Boiling fish is common in the North. The Indians boil it with a little flour, or broil oily fish like trout. Only white men resort to the frying pan.

In his novel "The Strange One" Fred Bodsworth, writer and naturalist, detailed a more traditional method of making a bannock:

Kanina's mother threw several pieces of wood on the hot coals in the stove and began preparing a bannock. Her hands were smeared with black gum from the balsam boughs but she didn't wash them. She opened a large bag of flour that stood by the tent wall and in the surface of the flour at the top of the bag she scooped out a hole about twice the size of her fist. Into this she poured a cupful of water and began stirring it with a finger. The water absorbed flour, grew pasty and she added a sprinkling of baking powder, pouring it straight from the can. She continued mixing it within the flour bag until she could lift out a round lump of dough that was ready now for the stove without a utensil having been used. She greased the frying pan heavily, patted the dough into it and placed it on the stove to fry slowly.

She smoked her little curved-stem pipe constantly and her rubber boots scuffed on the flour as she shuffled about. A large black pot on the stove began bubbling vigorously, its tin lid bouncing and releasing little puffs of steam. Kanina got a peek into the pot once when her mother lifted the lid. The liquid inside was yellowish and protruding through the thick film of grease on the surface was the carcass, apparently in one piece, of a small animal which Kanina took to be a rabbit. Water in another pail on the stove came to a boil and Kanina's mother threw in a large handful of tea leaves. There was no table in sight and Kanina wondered where they were going to eat.

Her father came back, grunted a few words to his wife and sat on the floor near the gasoline drum stove. Kanina's mother lifted the tea pail and the stew pot from the stove and put them on the floor. She took the lid from the pot and turned it upside down on the floor to form a plate, then with a large fork she transferred the rabbit onto the lid. Next she removed the bannock, now a crisp brown, from the stove and put it beside the stewed rabbit. She took down metal cups and a large knife from a shelf above the blue cupboard and filled one cup with flour, then sat on the floor herself. The meal was ready.

The traditional Canadian outdoor meal of bean-hole baked beans as cooked by a veteran New Brunswick guide is described by Dr. George Frederick Clarke, historian, archaeologist and angler, in his book "Six Salmon Rivers and Another". The setting is the famous Miramichi:

Several times he served us pork and beans cooked in a baker-sheet in a little tin oven. How crisp the top layer! and the pork, half lean, half fat, was ambrosia. Then, one afternoon, he dug a deep, wide hole in the earth and made a fire in it. No need for me to ask him what it was, or of his intention. It was a bean-hole. He kept the fire going for a couple of hours, then shovelled out most of the embers and ashes.

QUICK BEANS

Chop up ½ lb. sliced bacon and 2 onions and fry in your pan until soft. Fry 2 slices of bread, cut thick, in the bacon grease until brown. Remove the fried bread and add 1 tin baked beans. Cook with the bacon and onions until hot, pour over the fried bread and serve.

WALL TENT.

OVERNIGHT MUSH

Put 1 cup coarse oatmeal (not "quick oats") into a quart-size billy can with a tight lid. Add 1 tsp. salt and fill with milk or water. Let it simmer and thicken for about 20 minutes. Remove from the fire. Make sure the lid is tight. Wrap in several layers of newspaper and bury the package in a hole scooped in the earth. Cover with earth. When the tin is dug up in the morning, remove the newspaper and carefully shake off all earth. The oatmeal will have jellied and can be reheated and eaten at once. No more delicious outdoor breakfast dish exists.

A collection from old-timers and natives of B.C. compiled by Gwen Lewis, Buckskin Cookery, Box 665, Quesnel, B.C.

SNOW ICE CREAM

Catch a bowl of fresh snow. Sweeten with white sugar and flavour with vanilla. Pink colouring may be added or a tablespoon of instant chocolate mixed in. Children love it!

~ "Mama" Fowler

DANDELION SALAD

Dig up young dandelion plants before they have bloomed. Wash well around the upper root and the leaves. Cut up and toss with a wild onion with vinegar salad dressing. Young plantain and clover leaves are also good.

~ Mrs. Mathilda Kealing

POT PIE SQUIRREL

Skin and clean **4 squirrels** and cut in pieces. Flour and brown in good dripping. Add 1 qt. boiling water, **1 large onion**, minced, ¼ **lemon, sliced, salt** and **pepper**. (Fry the onion before adding.) Cover all closely and stew for 1 hour. Make a delicate biscuit crust, drop in rounds on the squirrels, cover closely and boil 15 minutes. Place the squirrels in the centre of a platter, surround with dumplings, thicken the gravy and pour all over.

~ Mrs. Jean Foster

Now he put into it his iron pot filled with beans and a suitable amount of salt pork, then, putting on the cover, shovelled back on top of it all the coals and hot ashes and covered the whole with earth. The following morning we had bean-hole baked beans. And what beans! No chef in all the world could cook any to compare with them. And flapjacks of real New Brunswick buckwheat meal made into a batter with canned milk, and then fried a beautiful golden brown. Then covered with butter, and lastly with maple syrup – that evaporated nectar which Gluskap, the friend and divinity of the northeastern Indians, taught them how to make long ages past. But I think I liked best the flapjacks covered with juicy baked beans. So did Bill.

A less palatable meal was described by Mathilda Kealing in "Buckskin Cookery", a collection of anecdotes and recipes collected from old-timers in British Columbia:

I thanked Trapper Joe for the meal and started to leave for home. As I passed through the outer shed, I brushed against something hanging beside the door. I turned and saw a freshly skinned coyote slowly revolving by one hind leg. Its teeth, bared in a flesh-less grin, gleamed fitfully in the twilight gloom. To my growing horror I saw that one hind quarter was missing.

"Joe," I called in a strained voice, "what was in that stew . . . we had for . . . supper?"

"Oh, you likum stew? Good, I tell you. Cuttum up coyote meat in little pieces. Put him in pot of hot water. Put some onion too. And some turnip and some potato. Maybe little bit old rabbit, or rice. Any old thing. And some salt. Boil him up good and. . . . Lady! Why you run away? You sick? Oh, lady, why you sick?"

The Ukrainian immigrant Gus Romaniuk, writing of settler days in Manitoba, recalled the time he shot a buck deer with his last bullet and cooked some of the meat, using mud and ashes:

We were hungry again but decided to wait long enough to roast the meat properly "backwoods style". I wrapped a chunk of meat in strips of birchbark and sealed it tightly with an inch to inch-and-a-half coating of mud from a nearby creek. Then I made a rack or grill by laying dry sticks across the hot ashes of our fire. The roast I set on these sticks, and built another fire on top of it. Meat prepared in this fashion cooks completely through in little more than an hour. When removed from the ashes, the mud is baked as hard as pottery clay in a kiln. We broke the baked mud away with sticks and eagerly sampled the meat. It was delicious. (It seems it always is when roasted this way.) Even though we had no salt or pepper, that old buck seemed to have taken on the succulence of prime beef.

The mud and bark "roaster" I used is not a hard and fast rule by any means. Paper can be used instead of bark, if it is available. We had none, so I chose bark because it is clean. Leaves are sometimes used as wrapping, too. I steer clear of them, however. Some may be poisonous, other types may impart a bitter flavour to the meat.

In 1945 Elsie McCall Gillis set off for a two-year stay at Arctic Bay where her husband, a meteorological officer, had been posted. In her subsequent book "North Pole Boarding House" she told how she kept house on the station and was faced with such problems as how to cook polar bear:

One day, there was a loud knock at the outer door. I went to open it. There stood Amoagolik, or Roger, the little old Eskimo who was the post trusty. His brown, weatherbeaten face was cut in two with an ear-splitting grin. He held out to me a pan of raw meat.

"Nanook," he explained. I knew by this time that nanook was the polar bear.

"From Jimmy?" I questioned.

"Yaa. Eehh, eehh!" he grinned.

"Thank you, thank you," I managed inadequately. At the moment, my two or three words of Eskimo didn't include the equivalent for thank you. Roger slipped noiselessly away.

I looked curiously at the strange chunk of dark stringy-looking stuff.

"However shall I cook that?" I wondered aloud.

My *Joy of Cooking* offered nothing on the subject of polar bear meat. So I sent John over to Jimmy for information.

"Cut it in slices about half an inch thick," the latter directed. "Score it well with your knife, then soak it overnight in vinegar and water. Takes away some of the strong taste. Then fry it in butter, add seasonings, like any other steak."

It still had a wild taste, I thought. And it was a bit dry and tough. But it was flavoursome and fresh, a good solid, substantial core for our Sunday dinner, certainly something we could get our teeth into!

Doreen Corps, who writes an advice-to-the-lovelorn column under the name of "Mary Starr", once described how she and her husband were treated to an Indian version of the most famous of all Canadian wild animals:

The children who brought it wouldn't say what it was – it was a surprise, a mystery! We thought we'd sampled most special northern fare. We'd eaten at lumber camps and savoured pea soup and baked beans that nowhere on earth taste as they do in a camp cookery in the northern bush. We'd had traditional French-Canadian dishes both at lumber camps and in private homes. We'd tried Indian dishes. We'd had stuffed pike, baked whole; we'd had pickerel and trout, fresh caught and fried in butter. I myself had cooked roasts of venison, plump partridge, succulent moose steaks – so tender you could cut them with a fork. But, no, said the children, our family never tasted this dish before.

So we ate it. It was good. It was delicious! But what was it?

"Tastes like roast goose," my husband said.

"So it does, but how can it be?" For there were no geese around at this season, and the cabin of the Indians, we knew, contained neither home freezer nor refrigerator.

But it was like goose. The colour and texture of the flesh, and the flavour, were almost identical. And the dressing surely, was the same dressing usually served with goose. Onions and sage, we could taste. My husband held out his plate for more, and I heaped mine at the

same time. The northern air gave one an appetite, and this, we felt, was a dish peculiarly suited to the country and the climate. We ate to repletion and beyond.

The children returned, eager to tell us what we'd had for dinner. But they waited for us to ask. And when we did, before Johnny had time to open his mouth, little Marjorie, her black eyes snapping, unable to hold the secret a moment longer, burst out with: "Roast young beaver!"

It was a meal we'll never forget. And one, until recently, we've loved to tell about. But my pleasure in roast young beaver has been a bit dashed. At a party the other night, after I had recounted the story of this most memorable meal, our host exclaimed:

"Good Lord! Our national animal . . . and she eats it!"

ARTHUR MAYSE TELLS HOW TO COOK A GROUSE OUTDOORS

Pluck it and remove the innards taking care not to burst the gall bladder. If your notions of woodcraft run to the romantic, you may now skewer it on a green sapling and broil it over a bed of coals. I don't recommend this treatment, because if the spit doesn't burn through, your fowl will almost certainly taste strongly of green wood. The chances are, too, that it will be charred on the outside, raw within and tough as all get out. Much better if, having disrobed and drawn your bird, you hack it up with axe or knife and toss the fragments into your tea billy. Parboil, then transfer to your blackened skillet for a quickie fry. Or you may simply let the boiling continue until you have a stew, which you will thicken with crumbled biscuit or whatever other bread substitute your pack holds.

Arthur Mayse, the British Columbia writer and outdoorsman, has considerable contempt for women who try to cook in the bush. Here he embarks on a few well-chosen words about the feminine way with freshly-caught fish:

Let us now, reluctantly, turn to woman's worst descent from grace when catering to outdoor appetites. I refer to her way with a trout.

You give it to her, daintily cleaned, its flesh pink and firm, cool from its nest of foliage in your creel. When she serves it to you, it could be just another slab of finnan haddie.

The desecration that any woman will work on a fresh-caught trout puzzled me for years. When the answer finally offered itself, it was, like the solution to so many of life's riddles, appallingly simple. To the female cook, a trout is not a trout. It is a fish and it says in the book you treat a fish thus and so. The book, most likely, decrees that fish be served with sauce.

I have indicated that a trout is not a fish in the ordinary sense of the word. Anglers will know perfectly what I mean and an attempt at explanation would be lost on others. "A rose is a rose is a rose," wrote the late Miss Gertrude Stein; and to filch a seeming redundancy from her locker, a trout is a trout is a trout. As such it calls for special handling.

Even in its preparation for the skillet, it rates respect. First with a sharp knife unseam it from the nave to the chaps – that, by the way, is a lift from another poet. Trout and poetry are all but inseparable. Then sever the neck behind the ears and tear off the head. The inter-bubbles will come away with it, leaving only the air sac and a dark accumulation of blood against the backbone. Scrape this out with your thumbnail, not breaking the delicately arched ribs with a knife point as women do. Dry trout.

He is now almost ready for the pan, in which you will have bacon grease scorching hot. Salt your trout's body cavity lightly, score his sides if he's over sixteen inches long, and roll him in corn meal.

Then into the pan with him, to crisp and sizzle first on one side then the other, till the dark-brown skin breaks away from the pink meat and his curled-up tail offers a handle to your fingers.

Here again, women lack the firm hand. They consistently under-cook trout. And, as we already know, they will, if not watched, serve trout with sauce.

BACON GRILLED TROUT

Beat and blend **2 eggs, 1 tbsp. milk, 1 tsp. dried parsley flakes, 1 clove garlic**, minced, **½ tsp. all-spice**. Coat **8 cleaned brook trout** inside and out with the mixture. Wrap each fish in one or two strips of **bacon** and place in a greased wire broil basket or on a hot greased grill. Cook over hot coals 20 minutes or till fish flakes with a fork. Turn once. Serves 8.

~ Roy Graves, Stampede Barbecue chef
for the Calgary Rotary Club

Doug Wilkinson, the film-maker who spent a year living as an Eskimo near Pond Inlet on Baffin Island, set out in his book "Land of the Long Day" something of the Eskimo philosophy about food:

One of the reasons for this is the difference between the Eskimos and white men in food taste and food pleasure sensation. With the Eskimos, taste alone does not play the same part in eating as with ourselves. They derive pleasure not so much from taste in the mouth as from the full stomach. No matter how much Arctic plant life you eat, you rarely feel full. It is a pure taste pleasure sensation. Badly cooked food, spoiled food, does not bother the Eskimo very much. With them I have often eaten food that has been in contact with kerosene and gasoline. I ate it reluctantly, because it was the only food we had. The Eskimos ate it with relish.

I like to taste food first, then have a full stomach; no meal is satisfactory without both. With Eskimos food remains in the mouth for only a minimum period before it is swallowed. A filet mignon as served in our finest restaurant would not interest an Eskimo. A half dozen such and he would feel happy; with a dozen he would be content. He would eat them any way they came, raw to burned black; that would not be too important.

Eskimos will eat odd combinations of foodstuffs, at least odd from our point of view. After returning south from my period of living as an Eskimo, I found myself much like them in this regard. It did not matter very much whether my meat was fried, boiled, broiled or raw, providing I got enough of it. It did not matter whether I started my meal with soup or dessert; it was all food and served the same purpose. I had not lost my taste for fine cooking, but it was not as important as it had been two years before. I am not sure that it ever will be again.

From *Land of the Long Day* by Doug Wilkinson, published by Clarke, Irwin & Company Limited. Used by permission.

PLANK-ROASTED SALMON— CAMPER STYLE

Cut a board 1½ inches thick and a little wider and longer than the split fish. Cover the board with foil. Nail the fish, skin side down, to the plank. Salt and pepper the fish and spread with butter, then prop the board at a slight angle near enough to the fire so that the fish will cook slowly. Brush often with cooking oil or butter. The fish will flake easily when done.

~ Roy Graves, Stampede Barbecue chef
for the Calgary Rotary Club

AN ALL CANADIAN

MENU

Oysters Canadian
Pea Soup
Brome Lake duckling with wild rice dressing
Fiddleheads
Young PEI potatoes
Mashed pumpkin
Blueberry whip with lemon
Oka cheese
Coffee

OYSTERS CANADIAN: Chop very fine, ¼ *cup* each *Lamb's quarters* (pigweed), fresh young *dandelion greens, romaine lettuce,* fresh *celery leaves* and *curly endive* plus 4 *sprigs* fresh *parsley* and 2 large fresh *green onions,* tops included. To this add: 2 *strips lean bacon,* fried crisp, cooled and well crumbled, *1 tsp. anchovy paste, 1 tsp. tarragon, 1 tsp. dry English mustard, ½ tsp. chervil, 4 fennel seeds,* well crushed, *1 tbsp. fresh chives,* well chopped, *1 tbsp. onion juice, 1 tsp. lemon juice, ½ cup bread crumbs, ¼ cup grated cheese,* a dash of *Worcestershire sauce, Tabasco sauce* and *Angostura bitters, salt* and ground fresh *pepper* to taste. Pound the whole in a mortar to the consistency of a paste, blend with ¼ *cup creamed butter,* slowly, in a blender.

Open on the half shell one dozen Malpeque oysters and cover each with the mixture. Top with grated cheese. Broil on a pan of wet heated rock salt for 10 minutes.

FRENCH CANADIAN PEA SOUP: Soak *1 cup of split peas,* yellow or green, in cold water overnight. Drain. Put in a pot with a *ham bone,* to which some meat is still clinging, together with 2 *chopped onions,* 2 *chopped carrots,* 4 *stalks chopped celery,* 5 *peppercorns, 1 bay leaf,* a little *salt, Worcestershire sauce* and *monosodium glutamate.* Simmer for several hours, or overnight until the peas and vegetables are all one smooth purée. Serve with crisp, crumbled bacon.

WILD RICE DRESSING: Place *1 cup of wild rice* and 1½ *tsp. salt* in 5 *cups of chicken stock* and bring to a boil slowly, stirring to prevent sticking. Then cook without stirring for about 45 minutes until tender. Drain and add *1 tsp. celery salt, 1 tsp. thyme, 1 tsp. sage, ½ onion,* chopped, *1 stalk celery,* chopped, *1 cup sliced sauteed mushrooms, salt, pepper* and *butter* to taste. Fill ducks lightly with rice, add ½ *orange* per duck and baste while roasting with red wine and orange juice.

MASHED PUMPKIN: Cook the pulp of one pumpkin until tender and mash together with ½ *tsp. dill, 1 tsp. cracked pepper, ½ chopped onion* and ½ *cup sour cream.*

BLUEBERRY WHIP: Soak *1 tbsp. gelatine* in ¼ cup cold water. Dissolve in ¼ cup boiling water. Mix the grated rind of *1 lemon* in ¾ *cup sugar.* Dissolve sugar in boiling water and gelatine. Add 3 *tbsp. lemon juice, 1 cup* lightly crushed *blueberries, 1 tbsp. Cointreau.* Chill until partly stiff and then beat until frothy. Whip 4 *egg whites* with ⅓ *tsp. salt* and whip into the gelatine and blueberry mixture until it holds its shape. Set in a wet mould and serve with Cointreau-flavoured whipped cream.

8

Towards a Canadian Cuisine

A display of Canadian cheese at the Colonial and Indian Exhibition, Imperial Museum, South Kensington, London, as depicted by the artist of The London Illlustrated News, *August 14, 1886*

The authors of this book recently took part in a heated argument with a Canadian gourmet on the subject of a distinctive national dish – or the lack of one. Our friend insisted that no such thing existed; we insisted that there was not only one – there were several. But whenever we mentioned a food or a recipe we considered Canadian in character he was able to prove, at least to his own satisfaction, that it derived originally from another land or else that we shared it with the United States and therefore it could not be said to be distinctively ours.

This argument we here reject out of hand. To say, for instance that *soupe aux pois* is not typically Canadian because other peoples also make soup out of peas is to say that ravioli isn't Italian because it derives from the Chinese *won tun* or that *sukiyaki* isn't Japanese because it is only an Oriental version of the Irish stews that Commodore Perry and his followers introduced into that meatless country a century ago.

Certainly Canadians don't hold a monopoly on clam chowder or maple syrup any more than the Jews hold a monopoly on chopped liver, yet only a confirmed hairsplitter would insist that these are not truly national dishes.

Apart from such hard-to-get game dishes as seal-flipper pie and beaver-tail soup, Canadian native foods fall into three categories:

▷ There are, first of all, the natural dishes, unchanged since Indian times – the Saskatoon berries and the boysenberries, the blueberries of the north and Bakyt apples of the Maritimes (so called because they have the transparent juicy look of a good baked apple). Maple syrup really falls into this category and so do those young curled ferns of New Brunswick called fiddleheads, which can now be obtained frozen. (They're cooked and served like asparagus.) Even more primitive, and perhaps more exotic, is Labrador tea, the brew the early explorers made from a small marsh azalea. From these and similar natural plants come scores of national pies, jams, desserts, dressings and sauces.

There is, for instance, a Mennonite dish called *schmier kase*, a buttermilk curd sold in the market at Kitchener, Ontario, which is German in its derivation. Mixed with sour cream and hot maple syrup (into which small doughnuts can be dipped), it becomes an entirely new dish, completely Canadian.

▷ Then there are what one might call the Canadian Species. Oysters may be universal; but there is only one Malpeque. Apples are grown in most countries; but the McIntosh Red belongs to Canada. There are dozens of different varieties of salmon; but certain Canadian ones – especially, we think, the St. John River salmon – are a dish unto themselves. Surely Canadian cured bacon is a distinctive national dish; why else would New York restaurants make a fetish of identifying it? The newest distinctive fish dish is the Arctic char; it is now easily available frozen. The oldest is the Winnipeg goldeye: a small undistinguished herring-like fish of the shad clan, it owes its flavour to a secret smoking process that belongs to Manitoba. There are some who would argue that our Brome Lake duckling is really just another Long Island, but there is a difference, albeit a subtle one: the Long Island farms are so large they decoy others so that the American duck has become crossed to some extent with various species. Ours is a purer strain.

▷ Finally, there are distinctive Canadian concoctions, many of them regional in nature and some of them derivative. The first was certainly pemmican, that nutri-

tious mixture of pounded buffalo meat and berries, which the early explorers used almost exclusively because it kept so well. Indeed, caches of pemmican recently disinterred from the prairie sod have proved to be edible after more than a century.

No restaurant today serves pemmican, but the pea soups, baked beans and chowders that enliven our menus are the lineal descendants of earlier, simpler dishes that the times and conditions dictated. Both beans and split peas were easy to carry; they helped build the nation. As for clam chowder, of which there are almost as many varieties as there are shells on the beach, it is easily as old as the country itself. Though Boston claims it, as it also claims baked beans, various varieties of both go back in Canada to the days before the Pilgrim Fathers.

A good example of a distinctive Canadian dish is the French-Canadian *tourtière* or meat pie, which came into vogue as the result of the prevalence of passenger pigeons in the early days. One of the characters in Ringuet's classic habitant novel, *Thirty Acres*, explains its origin:

"These pies are still called tourtières, though they're made with ordinary meat; nowadays it's just a kind of meat pie. But it didn't use to be that way. There was a bird they called *tourtes*, a kind of pigeon, and were they good to eat! They used to come along in the fall, whole bunches of them, like flocks of starlings, and the whole sky was just black with them. My old man used to say that when he was little and these tourtes showed up, they used to go out into the fields with sticks and just keep killing them till their arms got tired."

The best regional cooking is still to be found in Quebec, where it is easier to get a good meal than anywhere else in Canada. But there are pockets of specialized eating right across the country

from Saltspring Island in B.C. (spring lamb) through the Mennonite country of Ontario (smoked sausage) to Lunenburg, Nova Scotia (potato soup). Such traditional fare, adapted and revised over the years, can now be said to be as Canadian as sourdough biscuits or – well, as corn on the cob, for instance, a distinctive national dish which, like so many others, we have tended to call "American" by default. But corn was eaten in Canada by white men as early as it was eaten in the American colonies. Before the turn of the century – and later – the English treated it as *the* Canadian food, as this passage from the Empire Magazine of London, written in 1912, suggests:

"It seems a pity that more effort should not be made to popularize in England and Scotland the consumption of Canadian corn. . . . How many non-travelled Englishmen are there who have tasted roasted corn on the cob or corn oysters or corn as an accompanying vegetable to meat and fowl or corn in half a hundred different ways? It is a revelation. . . .

"Now Canada grows the very best corn in the world. Could not some arrangement be come to whereby a considerable quantity of the very best qualities were put on the London market and pushed by clever advertising? It might not be a paying proposition at first, but assiduity and initiative would make it go. It would add a new foodstuff to our daily life and could not fail to make itself liked. The idea should be well worth pursuing by business men."

The idea, of course, was eventually pursued and quite successfully. The only problem is that along with clam chowder, baked beans, blueberry pancakes, maple fudge, and almost every other Canadian gastronomic development with the possible exception of pemmican, corn in all its wild and wonderful variations has been kidnapped and appropriated by a more adventurous nation.

Drawing of the mammoth cheese by Frank Newfeld from an 1866 photograph.

Ingersoll's Mighty Cheese

Three years before Confederation, the Canadian cheese industry had its beginning in Ingersoll, Ontario, with the opening of the first factory. Indeed, in 1866, Ingersoll was able to produce for display the largest cheese ever fashioned by man – a mammoth production weighing three and a half tons. Ingersoll's "cheese poet" James McIntyre, one of the great unconscious humorists of his time, celebrated the feat with this ode:

We have seen thee, queen of cheese,
Lying quietly at your ease,
Gently fanned by evening breeze
Thy fair form no flies dare seize.

All gaily dressed soon you'll go
To the great Provincial show,
To be admired by many a beau
In the city of Toronto.

Cows numerous as a swarm of bees,
Or as the leaves upon the trees,
It did require to make thee please,
And stand unrivalled, queen of cheese.

May you not receive a scar as
We have heard that Mr. Harris
Intends to send you off as far as
The great world's show at Paris.

Of the youth beware of these,
For some of them might rudely squeeze
And bite your cheek, then songs or glees
We could not sing, oh! queen of cheese.

Wert thou suspended from balloon,
You'd cast a shade even at noon,
Folks would think it was the moon
About to fall and crush them soon.

RUB·A·BOO

Take **2 lbs. pemmican** and chop it up very fine. Put it in an iron pot, cover with water and let it boil for 2 hours. Then stir in enough flour to make a very thick soup. Serve hot on tin plates. This is an exceedingly nice dish for those who can spare the time to take about 16 hours' vigorous exercise after eating it.

~ The Canadian Economist, Ottawa, 1881

RAPEE PIE,
A FAMOUS
ACADIAN DISH

Boil **5 lbs. chicken, black duck** or **rabbit** in enough water to make 1½ gallons of broth. The meat should not be completely cooked. Remove the meat from the broth and break it up with a fork. Peel **12 large potatoes.** Grate them and squeeze in a bag, letting the starchy water drain into a bowl. Allow this water to set. Drain off the clear liquid and add the starchy sediment to the potatoes. Pack tightly in a bowl and cover it for a few minutes with a cold, wet cloth. Place the potatoes and **3 onions**, raw, sliced, in a warm dish. Add the boiling broth gradually, beating constantly, and season with ¼ **tsp. thyme**, ¼ **tsp. savory** and **salt** and **pepper** to taste. Put in a dish previously greased with hot, melted lard. Place one layer of potatoes, one layer of hot meat and one layer of potatoes. Bake in a hot oven, 500°, for 10 minutes, then reduce the temperature to 300° for 1 hour. Grease the top with **2 or 3 tsps. pure lard** and brown. Serves 12.

RASPBERRY VINEGAR

Cover **1 qt. raspberries** with a mixture of **vinegar** and water and let stand overnight. Strain the following morning. To one cup of juice add ¾ **cup sugar**. Boil and seal. Add this in small quantities to water for a cooling summer drink.

~ Buckskin Cookery, B.C., 1957

In "Pathfinding on Plain and Prairie", published in 1898, John McDougall described how pemmican was made from the shoulders and sinew pieces of buffalo, which had first been cut into flakes and then hung on stagings of clean poles to dry in the wind and sun for several days:

We made a large gridiron by digging a long grave-like hole in the ground, in which we made a fire and across the top of it placed willows, whereon we spread the meat. After cooking it carefully and thoroughly it was put away to cool, and then pounded by flail until it became pulp. This when finished was termed pounded meat.

In the meantime all the tallow or hard fat of the animal killed was cut up into small pieces and cooked or rendered, and watched closely that it might not burn. This boiling tallow was then poured upon the pounded meat, about pound for pound, and the mass thoroughly stirred up until all the meat was saturated with the hot grease.

Bags were made of the hide, nicely fleshed and prepared, and sewed with sinew. And now the hot mass of meat and grease was shovelled into the bags. Then these were quickly sewed up, and a level piece of ground was chosen, or a flooring of side-boards from the carts made, and these bags were placed on this and shaped and turned until cool and hard. A bag thirty inches long, eighteen wide and eight thick would weigh from 120 to 135 lbs. This was hard grease pemmican. Sometimes dried berries, or the chokecherry, would be mixed with the soft fat pemmican, and this would be called berry pemmican. This pemmican, like the dried meat, without any spice or seasoning other than sun and wind or fire, would keep for years in a fresh wholesome state.

George Frederick Clark, the author, historian and outdoorsman, described, in 1927, his introduction to Labrador tea:

On my first trip into central New Brunswick I was several months in the deep woods. We got out of tea. It was a tragedy until the Indians brought in some spicy smelling leaves they'd picked along the edge of the lake. They steeped them as we do tea and the liquor was not bad. It was my first acquaintance with Labrador tea – a shrub very abundant in Labrador and found along lakeshores and dead waters in this province. Save for a slightly narcotic effect it was a fair substitute for tea. But we were all glad when a party after moose came along and kindly gave us some of the real article.

In 1954, James Bannerman made a pilgrimage to an authentic Canadian monument and delivered himself of this report:

The little Ontario village of Dundela is tucked away in the upper St. Lawrence Valley, a few miles inland from the river near Prescott. The general store and the handful of houses are grouped together at a crossroads, with a placid air of having wandered there to graze on their own front lawns. Passing motorists drive through the whole place in less than a minute and seldom notice that what appears to be the village war memorial is a monument to a tree.

It was put up more than forty years ago by people who wanted to mark the spot where John McIntosh, clearing land for a farm in 1811, found a young apple tree growing wild, a tree with fruit that was honey-sweet yet delicately sharp, tender but crisp, with a glowing crimson skin and cool white flesh that smelled faintly of blossoms. From that tree, a chance-grown miracle, have come the millions of trees which now bear the annual harvest of McIntosh Reds – the best-loved apple in Canada and, with the Delicious, one of the two most famous apples in the world.

Sixty years ago the McIntosh had hardly been heard of beyond Dundela. Now, outdistancing such rivals as the Jonathan, the Snow, the Spy, and even the proud Delicious, it has edged out dozens of other kinds of apples from the Annapolis Valley to the Okanagan, swept triumphantly over the border into the United States and across the Atlantic to Europe, and is almost as well known a Canadian product as wheat and bacon.

Yet nobody knows how this horticultural marvel first came into being, or how it happened to be growing on the land John McIntosh took up in Dundela when Ontario was still Upper Canada and Toronto was Muddy York.

Fred Bodsworth, the naturalist writer, once visited the Paddock Tavern in Toronto to get this description from the chef, Andrew Costeck, of the correct way to cook a Winnipeg goldeye:

Costeck pushed his chef's cap back until a ribbon of blond hair emerged and declared: "You can't cook goldeye like any old fish, you know. You have to preserve and bring out the flavour that the smoking has given it. Mostly, goldeye are broiled, but sometimes pan-fried or steamed."

Costeck slapped a chunk of butter half as big as your fist in a thick polished broiling pan, waited until the butter was sputtering. He poured lemon juice over a goldeye and dropped it into the pan.

"This way the fish stays solid," he explained. "Goldeye get soft pretty easy. If you're pan-frying goldeye use a heavy pan or you drive out the smoke flavour. A thick pan slows down the heat. That's what you want to keep in the flavour and hold them solid."

In this passage, from "The Nymph and the Lamp", Thomas Raddall, the Nova Scotia novelist and historian, has a few warm words for some humble native dishes:

Within a week the station had settled into its new routine like the sand on the dunes after a flurry of wind from an unexpected quarter. As most of the food came in tins, even the butter, Isabel found the art of cooking simple. With the aid of Vedder's book, and after a few unfortunate experiments, she managed to bake tolerable bread and biscuits and to achieve an occasional cake or pie. Only the boxes of dried codfish and salt herrings baffled her. The author of the cookbook apparently had been above such lowly fare, and it was Matthew who showed her how to prepare chowder, and salt codfish fried with pork scraps or shredded and mixed with mashed potato

BRITISH COLUMBIA SALMON AND OYSTER CASSEROLE

(As devised by the authors on Gabriola Island, Gulf of Georgia, July, 1962)

Pick several dozen oysters off the beach and shell them. Place a layer in a large oven-casserole. Fillet one freshly caught salmon and lay it on the mattress of oysters. Chop up **2 hard-boiled eggs** and **½ cup mushrooms** and mix into a sauce with **½ cup oyster liquid** and **½ cup milk**. Pour this over the salmon, then cover with the remainder of the oysters. Cover the whole with **cracker crumbs** and cover the cracker crumbs with grated **cheddar cheese**. Bake in a medium oven for about 30 minutes until crust is brown.

CURRIED FILLETS OF ARCTIC CHAR

Cut **4 lbs. char fillets** into serving-sized portions and season. Sauté **½ pint chopped onions** and **½ pint chopped celery** in **¼ lb. butter** until tender. Stir in **¾ tbsp. salt, 1 pinch pepper,** and **½ tsp. curry powder.** Blend in **½ cup flour** and cook and stir until the mixture is very thick. Then add **½ cup white wine.** Spread two-thirds of the sauce in a greased baking pan and cover with the fish fillets. Top with the remaining sauce. Bake in a 500° oven until the fish flakes easily when tested with a fork. Garnish with lemon and parsley. Serves 12.

~ adapted from a Department of Northern Affairs recipe

COQUILLES ESKIMO

Mix **1 lb. flakes of boiled Arctic char** (skinless and boneless) with **1 pint white wine sauce.** Season with **1 tsp. salt, 1 tsp. pepper, 1 tsp. lemon juice** and **1 tsp. Tabasco sauce.** Mash enough **boiled potatoes** with **egg yolks** and melted **butter** to fill 2 cups. Make a ring of these Duchesse potatoes around the rim of each of six scallop shells, using a pastry bag, and then fill with the fish flakes. Cover each shell with **1 tbsp. Hollandaise sauce** and grated **Parmesan cheese.** Glaze in a 350° oven until golden brown. Serve on individual salad plates and garnish with lemon wedges and parsley. Serves 6.

~ as served at The Queen Elizabeth Hotel, Montreal

and fried in cakes, and the simple dish of boiled salt herrings and potatoes that he so strangely loved. He told her once, "I used to say, after I got away to sea, that herring-and-potatoes drove me away from Newfoundland; but it wasn't true, and there's been many a time since when I'd have given a day's pay just for a dish of 'em."

DR. BEST'S FISH CHOWDER

First, catch a **6-lb. haddock**, preferably from the Bay of Fundy. Remove head and tail and cook slowly in a small amount of water (2 or 3 cups) for about 25 minutes. Remove the fish. Skin, bone and flake it. To the fish broth add **2 cups boiling water, 4 cups cubed potatoes** and cook until tender but not soft. While the potatoes are cooking put **½ cup diced salt pork** in a skillet and when almost crisp add **2 onions**, sliced, and cook until brown. To the fish broth and potatoes add the flaked fish, pork and onions plus **4 cups scalded milk** and **3 tbsps. butter**. **Salt** to taste (we allow our guests to add their own pepper). It is preferable to make the chowder an hour or two before serving, refrigerate, then reheat but **do not boil**. Serves 8.

Authors' note: This or any other chowder can be improved by adding **1 tbsp. curry powder** to the fish broth and **1 tbsp. brandy** per plateful added at the last moment.

DR. BEST'S GREEN APPLE PIE

This can be used either for a shallow pie or a deep-dish pie.
Peel, core and thinly slice the number of **green apples** you need to fill to overflowing the pan or dish you plan to use. Apples shrink and if you don't want your deep-dish pie to collapse in the centre, an inverted egg cup will hold up the pastry. For an 8-inch pan, mix together **⅔ cup white sugar, ¼ tsp. salt, 1 tsp. cinnamon** and **½ tsp. nutmeg**. Sprinkle over the apples and add **2 heaping tsps. butter**. Cover with pastry and slit at the centre for steam to escape. Cook at 400° for 50 minutes. Put tinfoil beneath the dish to catch any drips. Serve hot. (Sometimes we add **¼ cup cranberries** for a touch of colour. A sprinkling of **dried raisins** on the fruit will also give a delicious flavour.)

Dr. Charles Best, the co-discoverer of insulin, is another confirmed devotee of the shore dinner. Here he describes the kind of meal he likes to enjoy on a clear September evening beside a towering driftwood fire on the beach at Passamaquoddy Bay, New Brunswick, at half tide:

On such occasions we usually start with clams, which we have dug earlier in the day, at low tide. These are steamed in seaweed and, to our family, it would be difficult to imagine anything more delicious as an hors d'oeuvre than these small clams eaten with melted butter and vinegar – about two dozen per person. The clams are followed by a steaming fish chowder (which I modestly claim as my own specialty). This is made with fresh haddock fillets from the bay, potatoes, onions, a little salt pork (these are usually combined the night before) and milk, which is added just before serving. Just short of the boil, the chowder is served in bowls to each of which a little butter has been added. Pilot biscuits may be passed around – but the chowder is a meal in itself. Even so, we usually look forward to the green-apple pie (made by a family expert) topped with a piece of old Canadian Cheddar which is our next course. The coffee is always made in open kettles over the fire and we are glad to sink back with our pottery mugs full to the brim with a satisfying brew to which salt spray and bits of charred driftwood have added a wonderful but indescribable flavour.

On the opposite coast, one of the native favourites is spring lamb raised in the salt air of the meadow-carpeted Gulf Islands of the Strait of Georgia. Here, Vivienne Charlton Chadwick describes how the residents of Saturna Island lure more than a thousand visitors every year with a Dominion Day feast of barbecued lamb:

When wind and weather are as they should be on Dominion Day, there drifts across the bright waters off Saturna Island a delectable aroma. This is the famous barbecued lamb with which the island's twenty-four families lure to their shores each year upwards of a thousand eager, hungry visitors. . . .

The day preceding the event is hectic. The men handle the butchering of some thirty lambs and the laying of a huge open fire about fifteen feet in diameter. Around the perimeter of this, leaning inward to the heat, metal spits will be spaced, each carrying a whole carcass. The women prepare the balance of the meal: Spanish rice, cole slaw salad, tea, coffee and cookies. The Spanish dish involves about seventy pounds of rice, dozens of pounds of tomatoes, whole sacks of onions, and assorted condiments. This is pre-cooked in various homes, set out in great pots topped with grated cheese, and left ready for the ovens on the morrow.

At five a.m. on July 1 the fire is lit. As soon as it has died down to a bed of pulsing coals, the barbecue team stakes out the lambs. Two men are required to keep the fire exactly as it should be, and two more to baste the meat with its very special sauce.

By two o'clock the Big Moment is approaching. The hostesses line up behind counters loaded with bowls of steaming rice, green salad, and platters of rolls. And around the dying fire, in white aprons and tall hats, armed with sharp knives and clean scrubbed serving-boards, stand the high priests of the Barbecue. A charmingly good-tempered line of a thousand hungry people from every walk of life is already serpentining across the meadow. They pick up large paper plates, file past the serving women, and wind up at the brown, crisp, tender Smoking Desire which is the day's *pièce de resistance*.

You may have your lamb cut from where you please, and you may have as much as you can eat. You take your heaped plate to the grass beneath a vast shady maple, and a blissful silence descends. The lamb is fabulous. More than one of British Columbia's lieutenant-governors have brought parties to Saturna Island on the gubernatorial yacht, and sat on the grass happily gnawing short-ribs on Dominion Day.

No more eloquent tribute to the mushrooms found in Canadian meadows has been written than that which appeared in Sheila Burnford's collection of essays "The Fields of Noon":

I am also fortunate that my home in northwest Ontario is within ten or fifteen minutes' easy reach of pastureland, bush trails, hill and lakeshore country – even if I only have six snowfree months to enjoy it in – and consequently there is a wide indigenous range of specimens. But all sections of the country, right across the continent, have their own special varieties; and even the city enthusiast can find endless possibilities in gardens, parks, and waste lots: that bane of the gardener, the "fairy ring" on his velvet lawn, is made up of the little bell-shaped Champignons (Marasmus oreades) – excellent in omelettes and stews, or fried; the supply is available from summer to fall, and taste even better in winter, as they dry particularly well. There are puffballs on lawns and golf courses; some of the short-lived stately Inky Caps (Coprinus) grow extensively on well-fertilized lawns, or from invisible stumps or roots under the ground – our best crop in this city comes from the lawns surrounding the Law Courts; and the unmistakable Shaggymane, or Coprinus comatus, barrel-shaped when closed, then expanding to a graceful bell, is often found along the roadside in tightly packed soil, or in the lanes dividing back yards in cities. These are the mushrooms that dissolve into an unsightly black mess, and because they are so soft and ephemeral should be picked in the barrel stage and eaten at once if possible: steamed is best with this consistency, or included in a casserole with breadcrumbs and cheese (and if cast away on a desert island one can use the inky fluid that contains the spores for writing one's S.O.S. in a bottle – it is remarkably unfadable). All the family of Coprinus are edible and good – but until one learns to distinguish the one called atramentarius, which is really quite easy, it is best to avoid alcohol when eating them, or for some time after, for the combination sometimes produces a hectic flush, fading very soon, but leaving a temporarily pink-tipped nose and ear lobes; this interesting manifestation soon fades too, but another drink

Coprinus atramentarius — INKY CAP

Russula variata

Pleurotus sapidus — OYSTER

Russula abietina

Six uses for maple syrup

HAM STEAK

Rub a **2-inch thick ham steak** with **mustard**. Place it in a baking pan and cover it with **maple syrup**. Bake for 2 hours. The meat should fall away from the fork like pie crust.

BAKED APPLE

Carefully peel and core an apple. Fill the core cavity with equal quantities of **butter** and **maple syrup** to which a few **raisins** and a dash of **cinnamon** have been added. Bake and serve hot.

RUM TODDY

Into a heated crockery mug pour **2 oz. dark rum**, **1 tbsp. maple syrup**, **1 tsp. butter**, **1 tsp. lemon juice** and a pinch each of powdered **cloves**, **nutmeg**, **cinnamon** and **ginger**. Fill with boiling water, stir and serve.

RUM COOLER

In a tall glass, filled with ice cubes, pour in **2 oz. white rum**, **1 tbsp. maple syrup** and **1 tbsp. lemon juice**. Fill to the top with iced tea and serve.

MAPLE MOUSSE

Pour **1 cup maple syrup** into a saucepan and stir in the beaten **yolks of 4 eggs**, heat until thick, being careful not to burn. Remove from fire and chill, then mix gently with **1 pint of cream** whipped stiff. Turn into a mould and refrigerate until cold.

~ adapted from The Royal Victoria Cook Book, 1900

MAPLE SYRUP PIE

Boil **1 cup maple syrup** with **½ cup water** (already boiling) for 5 minutes. Mix **3 tbsps. cornstarch** with **3 tbsps. cold water** and use it to thicken the boiling syrup. Add **1 tbsp. butter**. Pour the mixture into an 8-inch pie plate lined with pastry. Sprinkle to taste with chopped nuts. Cover with pastry. Bake in a 400° oven until the pie is golden brown—about 30 minutes. Serves 6.

~ Mrs. Arnold Heeney, wife of the Canadian Ambassador to Washington, D.C., in the Congressional Club Cook Book, 1961

within twenty-four hours or so will produce the same Rudolph effect all over again. It is not in any way dangerous, just embarrassing – some of the proprietary medicines used in combating alcoholism work on the same synergic principles of toxicology. It does not seem to work with everybody – both Susan and I have tried the combination without any interesting results. The city mushroom hunter may find the cool, sweetly scented brackets of that gastronomic joy, the Oyster mushroom (Plurotus), its colour and size varying with whichever hardwood tree or stump is its host. The variety that grows on dead poplar here is mainly pure white, and is conspicuous enough to be seen from a car along country roads. I have seen the brown variety in the elms around the high school here. Sometimes we sit on top of a hill in the country, and spot our oyster supper with field glasses. A small monkey would be invaluable to run up the trunk of the tree and throw them down like coconuts, for the fairest and the best, as with apples, are always at the top. One find of these shelving, scallop-shaped delicacies is enough for a meal, and they are heavenly, cut up into oyster-sized pieces and fried, with or without egg-and-breadcrumbs first. Then there are delicious Russulae, some nutty and crisp, some sweet and soft; and one, my favourite, that tastes of cooked lobster. Russulae are excellent for the novice to experiment with: an infinitesimal unswallowed nibble of the raw mushroom gives an immediate clue; the inedible specimens are hotter than pepper. Then there is the wide taste and consistency range of the "Sponge" mushrooms – so called because the undersurface has tubes instead of gills, and looks very like a fine sponge. The Boletus was so widely esteemed and used in Ancient Rome that it became almost a synonym for a mushroom; it appears as such in odes; and even the special serving dishes for mushrooms were called boletarii. I offer this snippet of historical information because recently I was interested to see that the contents depicted on a packet of dehydrated mushroom soup were unmistakably of the Boletus family. I have mentioned some of the obvious and easily distinguished mushrooms, with, to me, interesting tastes, but anyone with an eye perceptive enough to distinguish a dandelion from a daisy, the ability to read (and follow) an elementary textbook, and, above all, the commonsense to try no more than a mouthful of anything new can develop an individual list of epicurean delights – and benefit from the most peaceful occupation in the world while doing so.

John Clare, the Toronto novelist, editor and trencherman, is a confessed pickle snatcher. In this passage he recalls what it was like around his home in Saskatoon when the pickling started in midsummer, back in the 1920s:

Just to read the labels on the cans of condiments (bought from the Watkins man at the door) was like listening to a poem by John Masefield when his ship of poesy was running well before a spice-laden trade wind. Coriander, fennel, ginger, peppercorn and the best name of all, savory. As the bright mixture in the big kettle began to hump and the exciting odours of the spices were released the whole house was filled with an exotic presence.

It must have been about that time when I became a secret pickle snatcher. I didn't know it until years later when I was reading a magazine quiz which was supposed to tell whether you were a secret drinker. For anyone in suspense the answer lies in whether or not you take an extra peg when you're out in the kitchen filling your guests' glasses. It has always been that way with me and pickles. I often stop on my way through and take a spoonful of the clear golden joy that is corn relish or sneak a dill, free from the stultifying taste of meat and potatoes, which, I understand, are sometimes served by the undiscriminating with pickles. . . .

Our own storeroom was a wonderful place in the fall. The fine smells which had haunted the house benevolently through the late summer still lingered and as far as the eye could see stood ranks of "gems" or jars. Green-tomato pickles, one of our favourites, with peppercorn to be coped with like the shot in a wild duck . . . a crock of dills in one corner and in another eggs in waterglass . . . ruddy chili sauce . . . corn relish, its gold flecked with bits of red pepper. And there were always a few added starters on the shelves, the product of some trading or purchase at the Ladies' Aid sale of home cooking at the church. Some of these were frankly terrible, probably because they weren't our own. But one year there was a jar of tiny corncobs from the kitchen of a German family. I wasn't to see these again until a few years ago when I was in Kitchener. These crisp nuggets, plucked prodigally before their time, cannot help but make any true pickle man reach mistily for his bandanna, like a Kentucky colonel on hearing the band play Dixie.

It's that moment of rightness that makes all pickles taste a little better. The commercial makers understand this and run advertisements showing their men in the field equipped with walkie-talkies, and perhaps even stethoscopes, so that cucumbers, tomatoes and all vegetables chosen to become pickles may be taken at the precise moment of their rendezvous with destiny. When nearly everyone had a garden this timing was easy to achieve and pickling became a family enterprise, with the younger ones, who couldn't be trusted with the chopping because they hadn't learned the difference between an index finger and a gherkin, helping to bring in the fresh vegetables and clean them.

That way everyone, boys and girls alike, seemed to pick up a little pickle lore as well as an enduring appetite for them. In our family, as in many families, there are old cookbooks and old recipes, some of them so venerable they are out of fashion, unfortunately. Children used to be told to go easy on the pickles because they would make them dream. Some of these old "receipts" can start you dreaming just by reading them.

Ken Johnstone, the Montreal writer and gourmet, has been describing French-Canadian hotels and restaurants for English-speaking readers for more than a generation. In Quebec, he says, food is treated as "culinary pleasure first and nourishment afterward":

This divine dissatisfaction, which may well be the real secret of fine French-Canadian cooking, is not confined to women. I recall an occasion when Gaetan Major, a young Montreal advertising agency executive, undertook to show me how French Canadians prepare a steak. Now, when it comes to steak I share the chauvinism of most western Canadians (I was born in Olson Coulee,

John Clare's Favourites

GREEN-TOMATO PICKLE

Slice thin **11 qts. green tomatoes**. Add **1 cup salt** and cover with water. Let stand **25 hours**. Drain. Slice **1 doz. onions** and **1 cabbage** and add to the tomatoes. Cover with **½ gallon vinegar** and add **2 cups brown sugar, 2 oz. mustard seed, 2 tsps. allspice, 2 tsps. mace, 2 tsps. cinnamon, 2 tsps. ginger, 1 tsp. cayenne, 1 tsp. dry mustard**. Boil together for **20 minutes**. Bottle and seal. Makes **17 pints**.

CORN RELISH

Cut fine **9 ears corn, 6 cucumbers, 4 large onions, 6 green tomatoes, 3 red peppers, 1 bunch celery,** and add **3 tbsps. dry mustard, 2 oz. mustard seed, 1 qt. vinegar, 1 lb. white sugar, 4 tbsps. salt**. Boil **15 minutes** and place in sealers. Makes **6 or 7 pints**.

Pickle castors, in crystal or colored glass $1.00, 1.25, 2.25 to 5.00.

MME. BENOIT'S
OWN RECIPE FOR
LOBSTER A LA BRETONNE

Split a live **lobster** lengthwise. If you shrink from the job, have the fishmonger do it for you. Squeeze a **clove of garlic** onto the lobster halves. Now prepare the pan. For myself, I like to use an old copper pan because it shows up the beauty of the lobster. Put in liberal chunks of **unsalted butter**, then add **cognac**—follow your fancy with the brandy but don't drown the lobster. To this add a sprinkle of **rosemary**. Place the lobster halves in the pan and put the pan in a 400° oven and cook for 15 minutes. If you broil keep the pan 4 inches from the heat. Or, if you're a barbecue fan, wrap the lobster in aluminum foil and place it over the coals for 20 minutes. When cooked, baste the meat with the fragrant sauce. Then serve and eat immediately. If you're serving this for a party and you wish to give the plate a glamorous look, place a bowl of wild rice between the lobster halves on the plate. Flavour the rice with **saffron, chives** and **port**, and, of course, lots of **butter**. For extra flavour—and this is a favourite trick of mine—serve as a vegetable with the grilled lobster **1 lb. of thinly sliced raw mushrooms**, pouring over them when ready to serve **2 cups of onions** fried golden brown. The secret is to pour the red hot onions over the mushrooms. Add **salt** and **pepper** to taste. A dash or so of brandy never hurts!

about twenty miles out of Macleod, Alberta), who with reason regard steaks as a specialty of the west. In eastern restaurants we suffer the violations of good meat which are served to us under the name of steaks, consoling ourselves with the thought that it probably wasn't good western beef in the first place. But a French Canadian showing me how to fry a steak seemed to me at the time the ultimate in futility.

When I arrived at Major's home, he was in the kitchen and in a bad temper. "The damn butcher," he told me. "You can't trust them on the phone." And he showed me what looked to be a pretty formidable cut of sirloin, about an inch thick. "I asked for it two inches thick," he explained. Then he went to the phone and called the butcher, complaining angrily to him in fast and colloquial French. He came back and broke out a bottle of Saint-Emilion Bordeaux wine.

"Let's have a go at it just the same," he said in a dispirited voice. Then he took a sharply pointed kitchen knife and stripped out each tiny sinew and connective tissue, like a brain surgeon performing a delicate operation. He put a dry iron frying pan on the stove and let it get smouldering hot. He put another pan on a second burner and rubbed the frying surface with a garlic clove and dropped a piece of fat from the meat in the second pan. The fat began to sputter.

He dropped the steak into the first pan and there was a searing noise and smoke curled up as the meat hit the hot dry surface. He flipped the steak over, and then added butter to the fat in the second pan. He turned down the heat under the steak and poured off some of the steak juice into the second pan, into which he poured some Saint-Emilion wine with salt and pepper. This bubbled and thickened as he stirred the wine into the fat and butter and meat juice. Meanwhile he had sliced up a long loaf of French bread, set a couple of wine glasses at the table, and warmed up two plates over the stove. In a few minutes we sat down to a steak covered with wine gravy. The steak melted away under our knives, and we sopped up the tangy gravy with French bread. Again my thoughts went back to moments of youthful bliss and an ecstasy that I had believed long since to have been left behind me.

We were just finishing our orgy when the delivery boy arrived with another steak, this time the required two inches thick. We ate that too. I have never since disputed the prowess of a French Canadian with steak.

Scott Young, the Toronto columnist and novelist, once paid a visit to Mme Jehane Benoit, whose televised culinary lessons have made her the symbol of Quebec cooking to most of English-speaking Canada. Here he describes the experience:

I had lunch with her one day at her big home in Westmount, where she was born and brought up and where her parents lived with her until their deaths recently. I think what we ate that lunchtime came about in a way typical of her very personal approach to food. We had met a few days earlier in Toronto during television rehearsals. During one break in the several run-throughs between 1:30 p.m. and when the show was aired at 7:30 we were talking, naturally about food, and specifically about good ways of cooking lobster.

"You like them?" she asked.

"Very much."

"Then next week I will do lobster for you." She would do them, she said, *à la Bretonne*. She described it the way she talks food with every-one, relating it to a local culture, and travel, and people, closing her eyes and making a rapturous face to show how wonderful this way was. And she told me how she first had eaten it this way, one evening when she and her husband went to the Brittany beaches as the lobster fishermen were coming in with their catch. They ate lobster with the fishermen on the beach, without knives or forks and with folded news-paper serving as plates.

And so *à la Bretonne* was the way we had our lobster in Montreal with Madame's husband and a friend. But first there was a savoury of two layers of pasta made green by fresh spinach cooked right into it, the layers filled with chicken and tomato and cheese and baked in the oven. Dessert was a wonderful torte – a thick rich European cake filled with fruit or nuts – and cold fruit from an iced bowl followed by *café espresso*. The lobster recipe when she wrote it out for me later was as above, with a touch of her own sometimes swerving English: "Split a live lobster in two," it began. "If you are squirmish, get the butcher to do it. . . ."

The enviable cuisine of Lunenburg, Nova Scotia, has been influenced by the original German tradition, by the presence of Newfoundland and by New England cooking. Franklin Russell, the nature writer, once described it as "the result of a state of mind rather than a string of recipes." He spent some time there in 1958 gathering anecdotes to illustrate the influence of food in the Lunenburgers' lives:

One well-known cook, widowed a few years ago, received six offers of marriage within a week of her husband's death. Two former mayors once nearly came to blows in the main street, arguing about how Solomon Gundy, a local version of salted herring marinated in vinegar and spices, should be prepared. . . . This absorption with good cooking and substantial eating tends to make Lunenburgers bitingly critical of poor food. A German word, *lappisch*, meaning insipid, is still used to refer to tasteless food. A short, cheerful Lunenburg storekeeper, B. G. Oxner, once took home some Scottish oatcakes for his wife to try. His wife, Pearl, who is built on Wagnerian soprano proportions (the result, she says jovially, of eating all the right things), is one of Lunen-burg's best-known citizens. She served the oatcakes to a Lutheran pastor who was visiting. "How do you like them," asked Bertie Oxner.

"Well," said the pastor coolly, "when I want asbestos shingles, I guess I can always buy asbestos shingles."

The Kitchener writer, Edna Staebler, herself of Mennonite stock, here describes a traditional Mennonite meal, eaten in Bevvy Martin's sprawling fieldstone farmhouse near the Conestogo River in Waterloo County, Ontario:

Today it gives *drepsley* soup, dandelion salad and *fetschpatze* (fat sparrows)," Bevvy tells me as she puts on a clean print apron, tying it first in front to be sure the bow is even, then pulling it round and patting it over her stomach. I sit in the rocker by the kitchen window while she bustles between the sink, the stove and

LUNENBURG POTATO SOUP

Franklin Russell says that "this soup, despite its Spartan sound, can be made one of the most exotic of all Lunenburg dishes in the hands of a good cook."

Fry **2 cups cubed pork** or **bacon pieces** to a light brown colour. Dice **3 cups potatoes** and boil with **2 onions**, sliced. Add the browned meat to the pota-toes while still cooking. Leave 2 tbsps. of grease in pan and brown quickly with **2 tbsps. flour**. Dis-solve this in the soup. Season with **½ tsp. celery seed**, **½ tsp. thyme, salt**, and **pepper** to taste, **½ tsp. Worcestershire sauce** and a dash **cayenne**. Cook until pork and potatoes are tender. This dish, good in itself, makes a wonderful base for other dishes, especially chowders.

BEVVY MARTIN'S OLD-TIME SALAD

For each person to be served, fry **1 slice bacon** till it crackles. Take it out and to the fat in the pan, put **1 tbsp. sugar, 1 tbsp. vinegar**, plus **salt** and **pepper** to taste. If the sugar gets lumpy let it melt again and cook it all a little before mixing in **2 tbsps. sour cream**. Pour this over fresh salad greens and crumble the bacon into it. Garnish with a slice of tomato or radish rings.

FETSCHPATZE WITH MAPLE SYRUP

Fetschpatze are literally "fat sparrows" to the Mennonites, so called because of the form the batter takes when it is dropped into hot fat. The batter is made of **1 beaten egg, 1 cup sour cream, 1 rounded tsp. soda**, plus **salt** to taste and **flour** to stiffen to the consistency of bread dough. Plum-sized pieces are dropped into boiling fat and the result is dunked at once in maple syrup and eaten hot.

EDNA STAEBLER'S BEAN SALAD

Cut any quantity of **yellow string beans** lengthwise, French-style. (In Mennonite language you "schnippel" them.) Boil them in salted water until just barely cooked. Drain and cool the beans. Slice an equal quantity of **onions**, cover with **salt**, let stand 10 minutes and squeeze. Mix these with beans. Mix in a bowl **½ cup sour cream, 1 tsp. sugar, 1 tsp. vinegar, salt** and **pepper** to taste and cover the beans and onions. Toss lightly.

the big square table covered with bright-figured oilcloth. "You don't mind if I keep on working while we wisit," she says. "The curds are getting that smell I don't like round the house and I have to quick make my *haffe kase* (crock cheese)."

She melts butter in a graniteware kettle and into it pours sour-milk curds which have been scalded, crumbled and ripened for three or four days. She stirs the mass till it melts to the colour of honey, adds cream and keeps stirring till it comes to a boil that goes poof, then pours it into a crock and sets it away in the pantry. "Do you want to lick the dish?" She gives me a spoon and the kettle to scrape. "Some like it better with caraway seed in but we rather have it chust plain." Sampling its mild mellow goodness, I agree that it couldn't be better. . . .

At least twice a day there's a plateful of summer sausage. For breakfast there is in addition coffeecake, porridge or cornmeal mush and a bowlful of *schnitz* and *gwetche* (dried apples and prunes cooked together). For dinner and supper there is always a bowl of fruit, a plateful of cookies or cake, pudding and pie – besides soup and the main course. When I tease Bevvy about having three desserts she says, "Canned peaches are not dessert, they are chust fruit. Pudding is not dessert neither, it is only for filling the corners, and cookies and pie are chust natural for anybody to have."

On the stove there's a kettle of simmering beef broth, a pot of potatoes is boiling, ham is frying in a pan, a sauce for the salad is thickening, and in a pan of hot lard the *fetschpatze* are becoming a tender golden brown.

We sit around the bountiful table and bow our heads in a long silent prayer.

Everyone reaches for a piece of bread. The steaming soup bowl is passed among us and we ladle onto our dinner plates its clear fragrant broth thickened by tiny dumplings. Bevvy says, "Grossmommy Brubacher always told us *drepsley* (dripped batter) soup is especially nourishing for the sick."

"But I ain't sick," Sam's bright black eyes are teasing. "I guess that's why I rather would have bean soup."

"Ach, you like any thick soup where I sprinkle buttered browned breadcrumbs on," Bevvy says with a smug little smile.

"Except *rivel* soup," Amzie reminds her. It is made from milk thickened with egg and flour rubbed into *rivels* (crumbs).

"He eats that too if he has a slice of raw onion and summer sausage with."

"Ach, I eat anything if I like it real good or not, that's how we are taught not to waste," Sam says. "What soup do you like?" he asks me.

"Any kind Bevvy makes is so thick and wonderful I can almost eat it with a fork."

"More filling than the kind you buy in the cans, hah?" Sam holds his spoon like a sceptre.

"Have you never tried canned soup?" I asked him.

"We never bought a can of anything yet," Bevvy answers. "We always chust make our own."

George Spence, a member of the International Joint Commission, has described what he calls the greatest gastronomic adventure of all – western ranch cooking. The date is 1954; the place, the Q ranch in the Sage Creek area of Alberta. It's roundup time:

The evening meal was indeed a feast. There were big roasts of beef and lamb, cooked in their own juices – the ranch women know that no concoction ever invented can improve upon the natural flavour of good meat. With the meat course there were heaped-up bowlsful of hot mashed creamed potatoes. These were potatoes with that rich mealy flavour that only the glacial clays of the high prairies can impart, and each bowlful was crowned with a big chunk of butter that melted slowly away, imparting a creamy unbelievable goodness to the whole. There was a great variety of vegetables – green peas, string beans, young beets and carrots – fresh out of the garden, with the fragrance of the warm earth still upon them. There were bowls brimming with hot thick brown gravy, to smother everything in. Large platters stacked with sweet corn-on-the-cob – nature's packaged sunshine – were put upon the table boiling hot.

The secret was the freshness of everything. Once that pristine freshness is lost, no chef who ever lived can put it back.

There were fruit and vegetable salads to attract the eye and tickle the palate. There was delicious homemade bread – bread baked from the flour of the Hard Springs wheats grown on the open prairies, compared to which there is no other. And there were biscuits, browned to a turn, with that nutty appetizing flavour, hot out of the oven. Butter there was, not in miserable little patties, but in half-pound prints invitingly spaced.

For dessert there were huge wedges of crusty pie. Then, for good measure, the women placed upon the table big crystal bowls heaped with red succulent strawberries fresh from the vines, with the scent of the honey-bee's kiss still upon them. There was thick Jersey cream, which could be spread with a knife, to pour over the berries, and soup plates to eat them out of.

Then to crown all, permeating the whole atmosphere with a heavenly aroma, came steaming mugs of Mocha, the like of which the Olympian gods never tasted!

BAKED BUFFALO AND BEER PIE

Take **4 lbs. collops buffalo meat** (preferably from the leg) and cut in 1-inch cubes. Season well with **pepper, salt** and **sage**. Roll in flour and brown in a heavy pan in very hot oil. Transfer to a braising pot. Now cut up **3 onions**, medium sized, **3 stalks celery** and **3 potatoes** into ½-inch cubes. Toss these also in the same hot oil for a few minutes until they begin to cook. Throw this in with the meat along with the savoury bits in the pan. Take up the oil with **3 tbsps. flour**. Let brown in oven. Heat up **2 pints beef stock** or a broth made of any available buffalo bones or scraps. Add **2 tbsps. tomato purée** to it and **1 pint stout**. Blend this into the meat slowly and smoothly. Add an herb bag containing **1 clove garlic, 1 bay leaf, parsley stems, 3 cloves, 1 pinch thyme**. Simmer until meat is tender. Remove the herb bag. Turn the ragout into a collander to separate the sauce. Divide the meat and vegetables into individual fireproof pot-pie dishes. Correct sauce for seasoning and consistency, add to the meat and cover with pie paste top. Brush with milk and bake until golden brown.

~ Chef Edward Gebistorf, Hotel Vancouver, Vancouver, B.C.

BUFFALO STEAK AND KIDNEY PIE

Cut **2 lbs. buffalo round** into 1½-inch cubes and **1 lb. buffalo kidneys** into 1½-inch cubes. In a stew kettle place **2 pieces buffalo kidney suet**, about the size of a large egg. When the fat is rendered, remove the suet crackling from the kettle, add to the fat **1 large onion**, coarsely chopped. When the onion has taken on a little colour add the buffalo and kidney and brown them thoroughly, stirring almost constantly. Moisten with **1 cup beef stock**. Season to taste with **pepper, salt, a pinch cayenne** and **1 tbsp. Worcestershire sauce**. Stir well, cover the saucepan and simmer over low heat for 1¾ hours or until the meat is tender. Transfer meat and liquid to earthenware or glass casserole and cool it slightly. Cover the casserole with flaky pie crust and bake until delicate brown.

~ Chef Angelo Casagrande, Macdonald Hotel, Edmonton

An Intimate Meal for 2

DEEP-FRIED CAMEMBERT: Make a thick batter of *flour, 2 egg yolks* and *beer.* Beat *egg whites* until stiff and fold in and work in under batter. Add *salt, pepper, paprika* to taste. Take small pieces of *camembert cheese* that have been chilled, sprinkled with *hot pepper* and dipped in flour. Dip cheese in batter and fry in deep fat at 375°.

LEMON SOUP: Make a rich broth by simmering *1 lb. chicken wings* for three hours with *1 onion,* finely chopped, and *4 large celery stalks,* leaves included. Cool. Remove bones, skim and strain. Add a pinch of *poultry seasoning, savory, monosodium glutamate, Worcestershire sauce, salt* and *pepper.* Into each bowl squeeze the juice of ½ *lemon.* Garnish with lemon slices.

STUFFED TOMATOES: Scoop insides from *2 tomatoes.* Add salt. Drain. Sauté ½ *cup soft breadcrumbs,* with ¼ *cup chopped onion,* ¼ *cup chopped celery,* and pulp from tomatoes. Add ½ *tsp. Worcestershire sauce,* ½ *tsp. monosodium glutamate,* ¼ *tsp. tarragon, 2 tbsp. red wine, salt* and *pepper* to taste. Fill tomatoes with mixture, place in an oven-proof dish with a little water in the bottom, sprinkle with sharp grated *Canadian cheddar cheese* and bake for 15 minutes.

CUCUMBERS IN DILLED SOUR CREAM: Soak one thinly sliced cucumber in ½ *cup tarragon vinegar.* Add *1 tsp. dill seed* to *1 cup sour cream.* Add *1 tsp. minced onion, salt, pepper, monosodium glutamate* and *Worcestershire sauce* to taste. Mix and serve with garnish of chopped chives.

PEPPER STEAK FLAMBEE: In a chafing dish sauté *2 large onions,* finely chopped with *1 cup butter.* When onions are soft add *1 cup red wine.* Reduce the fluid by half. Force *4 tbsps. coarse black pepper* into two small thick filets together with salt, then sear quickly on both sides in an iron frying pan at high heat. Remove the steaks and cook them gently in the chafing dish with the onions and sauce. Heat ½ *cup brandy* in a small pan, pour over steaks and flame it just before serving.

Certain Reservations About The Future

In the October, 1960 issue of *Canadian Baker* there appeared an advertisement for something called an "emulsifier", this being an ingredient used by certain large commercial bakeries in the manufacture of what passes these days for bread:

"Plant personnel will like ATMUL 500 because it gives dry, extensible dough that won't hang in machines, clears the mixer easily, gives good oven spring. Your customers will like the fine grain, silky texture, improved appearance and lasting softness that ATMUL 500 adds to every loaf. Find out for yourself why leading bakers have switched to this remarkable product."

There, exposed in a full-page advertisement, are the criteria by which commercial bakers judge bread and bread dough and there in a nutshell is the whole philosophy of modern food manufacture: Efficiency, *si*! Flavour – who needs it? The word is never mentioned; far more important that the dough get through the machines easily! Texture, appearance and something called "lasting softness" (a phrase that perpetuates the monstrous hoax that modern mass-produced bread stays forever fresh) – these are the catchwords by which the chefs of the assembly line live.

A cursory study of the baking trade press confirms the suspicion that flavour is often the last thing to be considered in the bread business. Here is an article hailing a new bakery whose four standard loaves are described in terms of texture, colour, and the number of slices they produce, but never a whisper of what they taste like. Here is an ad for Wyatose Dough Whitener, which speaks glowingly of "softer, whiter, better bread", but never of better-*tasting* bread. Here is another heralding a new wrapping machine designed to "dress up" your bread for maximum "buy appeal". Doesn't anybody care that the stuff inside tastes like blotting paper and feels like Artgum?

The terrible example of bread ought to give us pause when we listen to the fireside tales spun by the food processors about the glowing future. It is easily observable to any man with teeth and a palate that, despite a procession of brilliant scientific break-throughs, the mass-produced and packaged bread that we eat today is in many cases far worse than the kind made a century ago by men and women who sweated before a hot oven. Does anybody wonder that the per-capita consumption of what was once called "the staff of life" has been steadily dropping?

"The trend in food today is convenience," the research director of a large Canadian milling firm remarked not long ago during a discussion about the future. His words were echoed by a packing company executive: "The day will come when the average housewife will select nothing but pre-cooked and pre-packaged meals." Boil-in-a-bag foods are already here; before long a housewife will be able to prepare a dinner in five minutes by dumping a dozen bags into scalding water. Bake-in-a-bag foods are just around the corner. By the time our children have children they will be able to press two buttons, one on a Super-Freezer, the other on a Super-Stove, and in less than two minutes, a pre-cooked, pre-frozen, pre-masticated meal will pop out onto the table. This is not whimsy. The know-how is already available.

Is this Utopia? The food processors talk as if it were. They speak, lovingly, of the new kitchenless apartments in which Mom, home from a hard day at the club, will simply press a switch and a set of giant machines in the basement will spew a variety of hot and cold dishes onto an automatic dumb waiter, direct to her table. When the meal is over, the flick of a second switch will send the garbage (including the disposable plastic plates) hurtling off down a special chute.

In all this forecasting, the assault against the taste buds is never considered. It is, apparently, assumed that every snack will be a gourmet's delight. Yet past experience ought to suggest the opposite. It is not only in the field of bread that we have retrogressed. In almost every area, from breakfast porridge to midnight coffee, from tomato soup to sponge cake, the flavours and textures which our forefathers enjoyed have been watered down, coarsened or cheapened by modern methods.

The simple example of orange juice, a standard breakfast beverage for forty years, will serve as a horrible example. There seem no limits to the ingenuity of man in creating new ways of processing orange juice. It comes tinned, tanked, frozen, refrigerated and dehydrated. But none of these new methods can match the original one. It still tastes a hell of a lot better squeezed from an orange.

Science, which has been busy of late developing plastic bottles to squeeze ribbons of baby food into the gaping mouths of weightless spacemen, might wish to turn some of its attention to finding a method of making canned, frozen or crystallized food taste as good as the fresh variety. When that day comes we may be said finally to have progressed.

Otherwise, if the trend towards efficiency over flavour continues, the future may not be the golden one the scientists foresee. I have already set down my ideas on the subject and since this is an anthology, may be permitted to quote from myself:

"The Art of Cooking, as far as I can see, is all but dead and is rapidly being replaced by the Art of Stirring. As a result, we have no further need for our taste buds and it is my conviction that babies of the future will be born without them. How simple, how efficient life will then be! There will never be any need to switch from Pablum.

"I can see it all so clearly. Each morning the housewife will mix up a large trough of Pablum before settling down at the TV set. Kids will take jars of Pablum to lunch at school. Businessmen, dining at the club, will have Pablum brought in on silver trays. At the cocktail hour, the hostess will float through the crowd with small portions of Pablum. At banquets, waiters will march in with enormous tureens loaded with delicious Pablum, coloured pink and green. At county fairs and amusement parks, Pablum stands will ladle out the stuff in cones at ten cents a spoonful. And on great festive days, the family will assemble at the groaning board to dig gratefully into heaping platesful of nourishing Pablum.

"How easy, how satisfying it will be! For Pablum is not only rich in food value but also it is of *uniform quality*, a point the food phrasemakers are always thrusting on us. One dish of Pablum tastes like every other dish!

"And it's so easy to make, too: no messy chopping, whipping or squeezing; no arduous baking, broiling, basting or frying; no sizzling platters or steaming saucepans; no unnerving aromas or pungencies to set the nostrils quivering; no crisp cracklings, soft hissings, bubblings or simmerings to set the glands salivating; no sudden gasps of delight to set the heart palpitating; none of these sights or sounds or mad emotions – only the thick, plip-plop of the Pablum as it slides effortlessly down the numbed gullets of a generation which has been taught that the easiest way to a man's heart is to just add water and stir."

In such a society of Pablum-eaters, or their equivalent, the true gourmet meal may be a nostalgic one. Encaged by panels of push-buttons, super-'fridges, readi-mixes, freeze-dried steaks, processed meats, ersatz beverages, powdered vegetables and crystallized Martinis, Mum may start to yearn for an old-fashioned kitchen and an old-fashioned chopping board. After all, if the scientists are right, time will be hanging pretty heavily on her hands in the Age of Automation.

Thus the true gourmet meal may be the kind of plain but hearty dinner that Harry Boyle writes about on page 69: a good rich soup, made from a real soup bone, with real vegetables straight out of a real old-fashioned garden; a real roast of meat, hung to your order and purchased from a butcher who actually cuts it to your taste while you stand over him; real potatoes, mashed by hand with the requisite amounts of real dairy cream and real butter; real gravy out of the oven pan, not out of a bottle; real berry pie made from berries picked that afternoon, stewing in their own juices beneath a coverlet of real pie crust, rendered light and flaky through dedicated rolling. This is the traditional Canadian farm meal and it has become a cliché to say, as countless farm wives have said, with becoming modesty, that there's nothing fancy about it. How ironic it is to contemplate a future in which this simple old-style repast may easily be recognized as the fanciest of all.

All the recipes in this book have been tested in the authors' kitchen. (Many, of course, are the authors' own.) Some of the early recipes, which come from nineteenth-century cook books and periodicals, have been slightly adapted to modern conditions; others are retained as written for their historical interest with brief notes by the authors suggesting adaptations. Recipes which the authors particularly like and recommend are marked with a √. Others, which are published for their curiosity value, but which the authors do not feel measure up to modern culinary standards, are marked with an X. In this latter category fall many of the early desserts and puddings — products of an era when the average housewife had at hand little more than flour, sugar and a few dried fruits. On the other hand, the authors were pleasantly surprised to find that a good many soups and entrées, long forgotten, were remarkably palatable — some of them even superlative.

INDEX BY AUTHORS

ACKNOWLEDGMENTS

Copyright excerpts in this book are reprinted with the kind permission of the following:

From The Bolton *Enterprise* by permission of Werden Leavens, publisher and owner; from *Early Days in Haliburton* by H. R. Cummings by permission of Ontario Department of Lands and Forests, Ontario; from *The Bruce Beckons* by W. Sherwood Fox by permission of University of Toronto Press; from a CBC radio talk by permission of the broadcaster, Miller Stewart; from *With a Glance Backward* by E. A. Howes, by permission of Oxford University Press; reprinted with the permission of Charles Scribner's Sons from *The Highland Heart in Nova Scotia*, pages 52-53, by Neil MacNeil. Copyright 1948 Charles Scribner's Sons and the author; from *My Canadian Journal* by Lady Dufferin by permission of John Murray, London, England; from *A Lady's Life on a Farm* by Mrs. Cecil Hall by permission of W. H. Allen Co. Ltd., London, England; from *By Track and Trail* by Edward Roper, by permission of W. H. Allen Co. Ltd., London, England; from *The Emigrant and Sportsman in Canada*, by John J. Rowan, by permission of Edward Stanford Limited, London, England; from *Newfoundland to Manitoba* by W. Fraser Rae by permission of Sampson, Low, Marston, Searle & Rivington; from *The Queen's Highway* by Stuart Cumberland by permission of Sampson, Low, Marston, Searle & Rivington; from the Montreal *Gazette* by Edgar Andrew Collard by permission of the author; from *On the Cars and Off* by Douglas Sladen by permission of Ward, Lock and Company, London, England; excerpt from the letter of George Tuthill Borrett taken from the book *Early Travellers in the Canadas*, edited by Gerald Craig by permission of The Macmillan Company of Canada Limited; from *The Imperialist* by Sara Jeannette Duncan with the permission of The Copp Clark Publishing Company; reprinted from *Anne of the Island* by L. M. Montgomery, by permission of Farrar, Straus & Giroux Inc. Copyright 1915 by The Page Co. and George G. Harrap & Co. Ltd., London, England; reprinted from *My Other Islands* by Evelyn Richardson by permission of The Ryerson Press, Toronto; reprinted from *Cabbagetown Store* by J. V. McAree by permission of The Ryerson Press, Toronto; reprinted from *North Pole Boarding House* by Elsie Gillis-Eugenie Myles by permission of The Ryerson Press, Toronto; special selection "Chicken for Sunday" © 1966 Harry J. Boyle; from *Made to Last (The Scotch)* by John Kenneth Galbraith by permission of Houghton Mifflin Company and Hamish Hamilton Ltd. London; from *I Married The Klondike* by Laura Beatrice Berton by permission of McClelland and Stewart Limited, Little Brown & Company, and Collins-Knowlton-Wing Inc. © 1954, 1955 by Laura Beatrice Berton and Pierre Berton; from *A Motor Tour Through Canada* by Thomas William Wilby by permission of The Bodley Head Ltd., London; from *Taking Root in Canada* by Gus Romaniuk by permission of the author; from *Land of the Long Day* by Doug Wilkinson, published by Clarke, Irwin & Company Limited. Used by permission; from *Northern Affair* by D. K. Findlay by permission of McClelland & Stewart Limited; William Morrow & Company Inc., Collins-Knowlton-Wing, Inc. © D. K. Findlay 1964; from *Arcadian Adventures with the Idle Rich* by Stephen Leacock reprinted by permission of McClelland and Stewart Limited, The Bodley Head Ltd., and Dodd, Mead & Company. Copyright 1914 by Dodd, Mead & Company; reprinted by permission of Dodd, Mead & Company from *The Strange One* by Fred Bodsworth, copyright © by C. Fred Bodsworth, 1959; reprinted from *The Wind and the Caribou* by Erik Munsterhjelm, by permission of the author and The Macmillan Company of Canada Limited; from *The Lonely Land* by Sigurd F. Olson by permission of Alfred A. Knopf Inc.; from *Buckskin Cookery* with the kind permission of Mrs. Gwen Lewis; excerpts from *Maclean's Magazine* with the permission of Maclean's and: Doreen Corps, Arthur Mayse, James Bannerman, Ralph Hedlin, Eric Hutton, Sidney Katz, Leslie Hannon, Hugh Garner, Hugh MacLennan, George Spence, Franklin Russell, Fred Bodsworth, John Clare, Kenneth Johnstone, Scott Young, Dr. Charles H. Best, and Edna Staebler; from *B.C. 1887 – A Ramble Through British Columbia* by J. A. Lees and J. W. Clutterbuck by permission of Longmans Canada Limited; from *The Legend of John Hornby* by George Whalley by permission of the author, The Macmillan Company of Canada Limited and John Murray Publishers; from *The Torontonians* by Phyllis Brett Young by permission of Longmans Canada Limited; reprinted from *The Diary of Samuel Marchbanks* entitled "Diary of Fireworks", Peterborough *Examiner*, May 31, 1947, by permission of the Peterborough Examiner and the author, Robertson Davies; from *Six Salmon Rivers and Another* by Dr. George Frederick Clarke by permission of Herbert Jenkins Limited, Publishers, London; from *The Nymph and the Lamp* by Thomas Raddall by permission of the author; from *Pathfinding on Plain and Prairie* by John McDougall by permission of The Ryerson Press, Toronto; excerpts from *British Columbia, A Centennial Anthology* by Phyllis Bryant, Vivienne Charlton Chadwick, Charles Frederic Morison and Rev. Jos. Nicolaye by permission of McClelland and Stewart Limited; from *Thirty Acres* by Ringuet by permission of the estate of Dr. Felix Walter and Mrs. Dorothea Walter; from *Driftwood Valley* by Theodora Stanwell-Fletcher by permission of Atlantic – Little, Brown and Co. Copyright 1946, by Theodora C. Stanwell-Fletcher; from *The Fields of Noon* by Sheila Burnford by permission of Atlantic – Little, Brown and Co. Copyright © 1962, 1963, 1964 by Sheila Burnford and McClelland and Stewart Limited.

Our thanks to The A & P Tea Company for the food shown in cover photo; to The King Edward Hotel, Toronto for use of Victoria Room; to Le Fournil, Bonsecours, Montreal, and chef Jean Guay; to Julie's Place, Toronto; to The Old World Cheese Shop and Jordan Wines Limited; to Mr. & Mrs. Robert McMichael; to the Canadian Pacific Railway; to La Société Coopérative de Povungnituk for the use of the graphic made by Juanisialuk "Caribou Hunter"; to Cameron & Co., San Francisco, for permission to reproduce cover from *Drinking Man's Diet*; to The T. Eaton Co. Limited for the generous use of their archives records; to Triangle Publications Inc. and Seventeen Magazine for permission to use cover from *Seventeen's Eat-for-Beauty Diet*, Copyright © 1962 All rights reserved; to Ogilvy Benson & Mather (Canada) Ltd. for the use of Metrecal tins.

Recipes in this book were reprinted with the kind permission of Mrs. Arnold Heeney, Mme J. Benoit, Mrs. Gwen Lewis, The Calgary Rotary Club, Department of Northern Affairs, John Clare, Dr. Charles H. Best, Edna Staebler, James Bannerman and chef Jean Guay.

Every reasonable care has been taken to make the list of acknowledgments comprehensive, but in a few cases all efforts to trace the owners of copyright have failed.

PICTURE CREDITS

Order of appearance in the text of pictures listed here is left to right, top to bottom. After the first recording principal sources are credited under these abbreviations: Bert Bell, BB/*Canadian Illustrated News*, CIN/*Canadian Queen*, CQ/C. W. Jeffreys from the Imperial Oil Collection, CWJ/Don Fernley, DF/*Handbook of Early Advertising Art*, EAA/Frank Newfeld, FN/Public Archives of Canada, PA/*B.C. 1887 — A Ramble in British Columbia*, RBC/The T. Eaton Co. Limited, TEC/Toronto *Saturday Night*, TSN.

Illustrations for this book commissioned especially from
Don Fernley, Hedda Johnson, Frank Newfeld and Barry Zaid.

Cover, Bert Bell/p. 1, *Canadian Illustrated News*, 1870/p. 2-3, BB/p. 4, Handbook of Early Advertising Art/p. 6, BB/p. 8, Hedda Johnson/p. 13, EAA/p. 14-15, BB/p. 16, CIN, 1870/p. 18, CIN/p. 20, CIN, 1862/p. 22, CIN, 1870/p. 23, CIWN, 1885/p. 24, The T. Eaton Co. Limited, 1899/p. 25, CIN, 1876/p. 26-27, Don Fernley; BB/p. 28, CIN, 1873/p. 30, CIN/p. 31, C. W. Jeffreys from the Imperial Oil Collection/p. 32, Rolph Clarke Stone/p. 33, Public Archives of Canada; *B.C. 1887 — A Ramble Through British Columbia*/p. 35, CIN; CIN; Montreal *Gazette*/p. 36, Barry Zaid from a CIN photo/p. 37, CIN/p. 38-39, DF; BB/ p. 40, Glenbow Foundation/p. 42, CWJ/p. 43, EAA; RBC/p. 44, Toronto Public Library/p. 45, CIN, 1870/p. 46-47, BB/p. 48, Toronto *Saturday Night*, 1887/p. 49, TSN, 1887/p. 50, CIN, 1874/p. 51, CIN/p. 53, CIN, 1871; CIN, 1871/p. 54, RBC/p. 55, DF/p. 57, *The Canadian Courier*, 1907/p. 59, EAA; The Ladies' Journal, 1895/p. 60-61, Barry Zaid/p. 62, BB/p. 64, TSN, 1887/p. 66, TEC, 1900/p. 67, TEC, 1900/p. 69, TEC, 1898/p. 70, *Canadian Queen*, 1890/p. 71, EAA; CIN, 1883/p. 72, EAA; CQ, 1890/p. 74, TEC, 1893-94; CQ, 1890/p. 74-75, TEC, 1900/p. 75, CQ, 1890; TEC, 1893/p. 76-77, BB/p. 78, Triangle Publications; Mead Johnson of Canada Ltd./p. 80, Every-woman's World, 1914/p. 81, Cameron & Co. Ltd./p. 82, Quaker Oats Company of Canada Limited/p. 83, M. D. D. Faema Co., Toronto; TEC, 1913-14/p. 84, King Features Syndicate/p. 85, Frank Newfeld/p. 86-87, CIN, 1863; CIWN, 1885; TEC, 1894, 1896, 1901-02, 1901, 1913-14, 1925-26, 1935-36, 1940, 1966/p. 88, 89, Pierre Berton/p. 90, TEC, 1913-14/p. 90-91, Robert Title/p. 92-93, BB/p. 94, RBC/p. 96, RBC/p. 97, RBC/p. 98, RBC; EAA/p. 99, TEC, 1899/p. 100, RBC/p. 101, FN/p. 102, RBC/p. 103, Eskimo Graphic Art/p. 104-105, BB/p. 106, *Illustrated London News*, 1886/p. 108, FN from a PA photo/p. 113, Dennis Burton/p. 115, TEC, 1893/p. 116, Toronto Public Libraries/p. 118, CIN, 1883/p. 120-121, BB/p. 128, EAA.

PRINTED AND BOUND IN CANADA

TYPOGRAPHER McCorquodale & Blades Printers Ltd.

PAPER Webcoat

LITHOGRAPHY Litho-Print Limited

BINDING *cases printed by* Sampson Matthews Limited
cases made by The Ryerson Press
bound by T. H. Best Printing Co. Limited